The Hobo Diaries

Down and Out on Martha's Vineyard

by Holly Nadler

For permission, serialization, condensation, adaptions, or for our catalog of other publications, write to Ozark Mountain Publishing, Inc., P.O. Box 754, Huntsville, AR 72740, ATTN: Permissions Department.

Library of Congress Cataloging-in-Publication Data

The Hobo Diaries: Down and Out on Martha's Vineyard
by Holly Nadler -1948-

You can idyll for decades on a gorgeous island, comfy, safe, and warm, immersed like a Medieval mystic on a life-long spiritual path, and all of a sudden it feels as if you've been dumped on a water slide with a sign that reads: This life is out of your price range, Splash!

1. Medieval Mystic 2. Spiritual 3. Homelessness 4. Depression
I. Nadler, Holly-1948- II. Medieval Mystic III. Spiritual IV. Title

Library of Congress Catalog Card Number: 2022938801
ISBN: 9781956945058

Cover Art and Layout: Victoria Cooper Art
Book set in: Jakob & Times New Roman
Book Design: Summer Garr
Published by:

OZARK
MOUNTAIN
PUBLISHING

PO Box 754, Huntsville, AR 72740
800-935-0045 or 479-738-2348; fax 479-738-2448
WWW.OZARKMT.COM

Printed in the United States of America

Contents

This is a memoir, which means it's been stripped, flayed, and marinated from real life. That being said, there are several personalities that require enough descriptive flavoring that they won't be recognized. I'll mark their first appearances with asterisks to signal a made-up name and a reimagined identity. Somebody told me, indignantly, that you can't fictionalize any part of a memoir. This person happened to be among the asterisk contingent. She—or he or they—will thank me one day.

1

The End of Days on Martha's Vineyard

I don't know what I'm doing but, whatever it is, it's gonna be all right. Or not.

See, I'm moving. The deal on moving, nowadays, on the island, is that if you've got a roof over your head, you hold on to it with bloody fingernails (which haven't been professionally manicured in years), even as the landlord who sold the digs out from under you is having you evicted by a team of draught horses. And why do you hang on?

Because you will *NEVER EVER* find another place, not a treehouse, not a shed, not anywhere on this five-star island.

After twelve years in two owned—yes, *owned*, cash-on-the-barrel-head—houses, a bunch of rented cribs stacked up over ten or so years, and a final eight years of fair-to-middling satisfaction of living in one place—a long time for a nomad—I gave notice on my apartment—rehabbed out of the old library in lovely, seaside, gingerbready Oak Bluffs—when every last woeful tale of so doing always leads to the poor dude finding herself obliged to move away, far away, maybe to some dusty inland county where she's lucky to win a job as a Walmart greeter.

I'm seventy years old. An inconvenient age at which to become homeless.

I don't even own a car, so that's homelessness squared.

So how did this scary situation befall me, I, who've held deeds to waterfront property on both coasts, who've written for

Laverne & Shirley, published books, and "inked" thousands of articles for local newspapers, plus magazines, some of them national? Ever hear of *Cosmo*? *Women's World*? *The Utne Reader*? *Lear's*?

What was the question? Oh! How'd I get so stupid as to give up my year-round Vineyard rental?

Could we chalk it up to family dysfunction without going into elaborate detail? In January I made a trip with my Boston terrier, Huxley, out to the Coachella Valley in California where my mother lives in condo splendor. She's ninety-eight years old and still navigating the stairs to her master bedroom suite. Downstairs, she cooks her own small meals. She still drives, for crying out loud. (Yes, take a moment to shudder at this point.) But here's the thing: her memory has slipped more cogs than her foot on the gas pedal. I agreed to move back to the west coast and take up residence along with my sister, who's been there for the long haul—she's the good sib.

Can you see where this is going? I made the fatal decision to give notice on my darling Vineyard apartment with its two spacious rooms under a mansard roofline.

Cue the horror movie scream.

◆ ◆ ◆

Within three weeks my sister and I were squabbling the way we used to do over the single Barbie doll our parents insisted we share. You know what else my parents decreed, this time to overtly hold her interests over mine? They gave her proprietary rights to the color pink! I love pink! But, no, I was forced to take blue whenever pink and blue choices arose. I mean, blue's alright but . . .

After our prolonged fifty-seventh fight out in the desert, I packed up a suitcase the size of a lunch box—I travel light— left my poor pooch for the time being with my poor family, and headed back to Massachusetts.

I love the island more than life itself. In 1984 I gave birth to my son here. From his second-grade school career onward, I and my beloved ex-husband Marty reared him on this blessed island. Now both of them have flown the coop, Marty to his late mother's condo in Florida, Charlie with his bride Cary to prestigious jobs in NYC, but I seem to be holding a space on the island for the three Nadlers from some long-ago pact that only exists in the abandoned mine of my mind.

The minute I returned to MV in the spring of 2018, two ideas were continuously pitched to me from friends and, well, not just friends, but from *EVERYBODY*, including my 2,200+ friends on Facebook:

1. "Can you rescind your notice to give up your apartment?" and . . .
2. "Have you considered signing up for senior housing?"

The second option gives me the heebie-jeebies. Do they suggest this because of the skin that flaps between my elbow and shoulder like a turkey gibbet in a rotisserie?

My friend, *NY Times* bestselling author Susan Wilson, opined in a recent email, "Just spitballing here, but have you applied to Island Elderly Housing? Ignore the fact that it's an off-putting name for those of us who will never be elderly, but it may be a solution, if not immediately, and it would be good for you to get on their list. Yes, they do take well-behaved dogs."

Spitball all you want, amiga, I'm just not ready.

It's not vanity. If I were vain would I have mentioned turkey gibbet arm flesh? Here's the thing so many people fail to understand, particularly those lucky enough to have an ancient affordable mortgage on their home, and a set of grandkids ready for ambassadorships to the great capitals of Europe: You've acquired your gorgeous lives by staying in one place.

Congratulations. It works great.

Wish I could have managed it.

And yet some of us have a gypsy gene that keeps us moving forward in a life of pure exhilarating romantic adventure.

It also sinks us into poverty, lost seaside cottages, failed marriages, and even—*groan!*—badly behaved family pets.

But I beg you, readers and spitballing islanders, follow me on my last hoist onto my camel in search of the next oasis. My next oasis on island, of course.

Yeah, I know. I'm fucked.

2

Rental Tragedia No. 1

It started out okay, as these things tend to do. How else would you willingly enter into what any normal person could see is a patently crummy situation?

No sooner had I started to pile FREE detritus outside my building—pots and pans, mismatched plates, a black-and-gold antique Singer sewing machine, even a few pink items I was finally willing to sacrifice; a scarf too thin to do much good in winter (and who wears them in summer?), a pink polyester seal-doll, good for hugs—when I fell into a network of other homeless cowboys.

Turns out we all find each other through social media, and the sheer numbers of other pals on the same highway to sleeping under the stars doesn't fail to alarm.

My newish buddy Lizzy Wallace*, poet, peace activist, artist, has been chasing down local rental leads, occasionally redirecting one to me.

Lizzy tells me to call the younger brother* of a woman* I've long known about town, a retired sports car racer who years ago made a name for herself on the NASCAR circuit. A fiery crash finished her career, and she came out of it with a prosthetic leg below the right knee and a foggy mental capacity that may have been a precondition.

Her house, won with NASCAR money, is sprawling,

attractive, if a little worn out. Scratch that. *A LOT* worn out.

It's tucked into one of the many dirt roads ending prettily at the lagoon on the Oak Bluffs side. Lizzy directs me to this woman's kid brother; he oversees his sister's rentals, and he's a fan of my local reporting.

I call him up one morning. He bubbles over with welcome. He explains that since big sister's accident, he's been charged with caring for her. Also, he lives rent-free in the upstairs master suite with a deck overlooking the water, so it behooves him to secrete t.l.c. like motor oil from a tin can.

His core value, he maintains, is raking in money for big sis during the summer months. This means renting out rooms to seasonal workers at $6,000, June through September.

My own budget is a fraction of that, but kid bro is cheerful and unfazed and, again, he loves my work. He'll rent me the sunroom, a more casual and yet charming facility with its own door to the outside world through which I and my elderly Boston terrier can come and go. For a woman who hasn't bunked with roommates since college days, this easy exit seems like making the best of a dubious situation.

"*Problemo* solved!" I crow to my pessimistic comrades who've practically thrownthemselves at my ankles to plead:

"*PLEASE TAKE BACK YOUR APARTMENT!*" or, as I previously mentioned: "*SIGN UP FOR ELDERLY HOUSING!*"

I find a nice broken-down bloke-about-town named Leigh Rogers, in his fifties, slim, with straight black hair and a determinedly blank expression on his olive-complected Azorean face.

He owns a beat-up white El Camino truck with which he'll help me get householdfurniture to big sis and kid bro's home.

Kid B, whom I haven't yet met, texts me instructions to pile everything behind one of the many broken-down living room sofas. For some reason, when we arrive on the scene, Big S is livid because Kid B hasn't consulted her. I think I can smell daytime booze wafting from white chapped lips.

Meanwhile, mercifully, the household's King Charles spaniel, Rinaldo, throws himself against me in a lather of affection. This makes everything okay. Pile on the animals is my own personal battle cry for all of life's challenges.

It's April 20, and I won't move in until June 1, but for a second drop-off of my things, Kid B demands a check.

Small as it's bound to be, he seems to need it.

Leigh and I bring over my pink-*PINK!*-stenciled-and-distressed-by-me dresser (my favorite belonging), books and clothes, and the daybed that's seen me through many a change in domicile. Per the check, Kid B's desperation makes me think he and Sis are out of eggs and English muffins and maybe even Cheerios.

I hold off on signing over any money until some kind of all-clear signal tolls.

When Leigh and I show up, Big S is at the door, fuming. She points to Kid B, a slim middle-aged man with a graying man bun. He and a younger, shy woman with a mop of curly dirty-blond hair, are busy tugging a double bed into the sunroom. Wait.

The sunroom?!

Over his shoulder he snaps at me, "I'm transferring you to one of the inside bedrooms." What happened to the guy who bubbled with welcome when I first rang him up?

But . . . but . . . my brain splutters. What about my strategy of an easy exit from therooming house? Leigh, who's beginning to seem like my only friend in the world, and I stow away the dresser and other gear in a dark back bedroom.

The one small window faces a brick embankment leading down to the cellar. Funny how, in this shadowy room, even the pink dresser emits no magic.

A few minutes later K. B. announces he and I will be sharing the bathroom across the hall. I joke weakly that this will help us to bond. He glares at me and I realize he's one of those guys who can *NOT* recognize a woman's humor. You'll find it in the DMZ.

At this point I seem to have as much chance of bonding with a bag of peat moss.

As Leigh and I chug away down the road, I learn more about him. I already know he's only willing to work for any one party for an hour at a time. More than that is a quantity of labor to which he cannot commit. I'm fine with his small jobs.

He tells me he used to be a town drunk.

He got in trouble for calling in a bomb scare at the Oak Bluffs post office. Now he takes his time, in one-hour work dribs. The Commonwealth of Massachusetts pays him to receive medication in two weekly injections. What's it for? I ask, perhaps tipping over the privacy zone. He shrugs.

"Keeps me from getting paranoid."

I give him a sidelong glance. In a white button-down shirt that actually appears to be ironed, he presents a pulled-together look. Not a bit paranoid.

And yet he's got an odd relationship with his sister, Camilla, short, plump, also black-haired, who pulls up alongside him, facing the other direction, at least twice during the allotted hour that I'm with him.

"LEAVE ME THE FUCK ALONE!" he shouts at her through their open windows.

She's unfazed. "What time you want dinner?"

I try to make sense of their family regs: Leigh lives alone in some flea-ridden shack down the road from the ancestral digs, but his mother and sister, who lodge together, put food on the table. I'm not sure how it works. As far as I know, he never misses a meal, but he's insanely curt to poor Cammy:

"Don't bother me! Don't follow me! Don't call me!" That's his constant barrage, whether Cammy finds him on a back road or rings him up on his cell.

"Leave me the fuck alone!" he rages at her. And yet, the following day, when I've hired him for another of our single hours, and when I ask him about dinner the night before, he'll snap:

"My sister made tacos!"

Or burgers or meatloaf. In other words, for all her bro's grumpiness, Cammy every evening takes a spatula and slides something from the pan to Leigh's plate.

♦ ♦ ♦

I wake up in my soon-to-be-defunct apartment, atop a bedroll on the floor, as 6 a.m. texts ping near my face. Kid B writes that he's having second thoughts about my new bedroom assignment. He needs the full six thou for his sister's bank account.

I text him, how 'bout our original plan for tenancy of the sunroom? Silence on his end lets me know his shy girlfriend is getting that room, conveniently tucked away from the rest of the household folks who will never hear the couple's torrents of lovemaking.

Whatever impulse had originally awarded the sunroom to me has now ceded place to the ferocious demands of L-U-S-T.

I've been celibate, seriously, happily so, for so many years, I can barely remember the steam engine thrust of L-U-S-T, and how it wreaks so much power over our decisions. All I can do is shake my head and hope this poor schmuck comes to his senses . . .

Texts can only go so far; I phone the dude, hoping to reason with him, but he lapses into full-out rant about me misinterpreting everything he says.

I cry out, "Please stop yelling! I'll have to hold the phone away from my ear!" See how tough I can be?

I position the receiver away, and he hangs up.

A final text orders me to *COME GET YOUR SHIT!*

My new best friend Leigh and I move all my personal belongings to the front room of the Book Barn, which I'll be managing over the summer (more—much more to come—about the deep dark haunted bookstore). I realize the owner* who lives abroad in Belarus isn't going to love having the contents of my lost rental piled in the front room, but I'm determined to find a new rental before the bookstore opens on our agreed-upon date of June 1.

Vineyard Shuffle 1 / Poor homeless lady 0.

3

Rental Tragedia No. 2

In the wake of the boardinghouse debacle with Kid B and Big S, I seek refuge at a dear old friend's place for a few nights of protective custody.

Lorinda* is seventy-six, tall and rangy, with a shoulder's length of self-tended silvery brown hair. She lives in Edgartown in a small captain's house once shared with her late husband, he a New Jersey headmaster of a well-regarded private school, she an art teacher retired from that same institution of High Preppy learning.

So there I sit as she puts together a nourishing meal of homemade vegetable soup and a salad with a groan-making amount of cut-up kale. I relate the whole frightful tale of the rental yanked out from under me.

Much as I need to, I make an effort not to weep.

You know how weeping works in our later years: most of us have learned from our stoic culture to keep it zipped. For me I can only cry over certain heart-tugging movies—*84 Charing Cross Road* comes to mind, with Anne Bancroft and Anthony Hopkins, she a smoking, hard-bitten Manhattan writer, he a rare books dealer in London. Also sad-as-heck songs like Joni Mitchell's "I Wish I Had a River to Skate Away On," which, thankfully, never plays on any radio station in the lower forty-eight states.

But there are other ways to cry. Your face gets red, even

slightly throttled, your larynx seizes up until only a few hoarse syllables emerge, and you take quick swipes at your nose with a napkin.

I sigh, then ask my friend in one gulp: "Could I rent an upstairs bedroom from you? For June? I'll be sure to find something else for July and August."

This isn't far-fetched. She routinely rents to off-island friends for a very reasonable amount.

"Of course," she says with consummate mercy.

See?! You can lose a sure-thing rental and find somewhere new to settle with the snap of your fingers. There will be no problem with me always snagging a place to live on my precious island. Right?

With Leigh's help, I hump all my clothes on hangers from the bookstore and salt them into the closet of Lorinda's gracious upstairs bedroom, replete with a den's collection of sofas and chairs, a desk, and a sweeping view of an emerald-green lawn where I know my Boston terrier Huxley, once I retrieve him from my mom's condo in California, will range freely like the deer and the antelope in that cowboy song.

I spend a couple of lovely nights at Lorinda's, and then I have one of those days that make you wonder as you tuck into bed some twenty hours later, how in the blue blazes you managed to pull it all off.

I call for a taxi at 5:45 a.m. I have plenty of time at the Steamship terminal to buy a bus-and-boat ticket to Logan Airport, and to worry about whether this would prove one of those Sound crossings everybody's been whinging about in Islanders Talk, with our beloved vessels stalling like potato peels in a backed-up sink.

For anyone needing to catch a plane, that just kills it.

Sure enough, about ten minutes outside Wood's Hole, the *Martha's Vineyard* ferry is suddenly dead in the water. We all look out at the gaseous wake swirling around the hull.

And then the engines start up again . . . whew! I text my son in New York: "On the boat!"

He writes back: "Amazing!"

Later I also report that the bus, too, although arriving in Wood's Hole half an hour late, is blasting north on Route 28.

He texts, "A miracle!!!" He's always been, from the earliest age, both sarcastic and supportive, an ambrosial combination in a son, though I can't quite say why.

Two plane rides later, and a pickup at the Palm Springs airport by my brother, Owen, a genial chap but a Trumper, for crying-out-loud-was-he-fucking-adopted?!—I intercept an email from Lorinda bewailing her own terrible guilt: her daughter, son-in-law, and college-aged grandkids have asked to spend a long weekend with her in June.

Could I please find another roof over my head, so sorry, SOOOO SORRY!

"I wish I could have been the one to rescue you."

Do you, Lorinda? What is it about rescue that drops off your heart scale? Could you have said to your daughter, "Of course you'll come, but we'll need to work around Holly's staying here, even if I have to put her up on the den couch; she's a good sport. If I don't put a roof over her head, she'll be homeless."

Okay, Plan C: Take my pride with a pair of tongs in my hands and plead on Facebook for a rental. Nothing fancy. In fact, here's what I write:

> This feels like committing hari kari in the public square -- well, Post Office Square, with the divine apple fritters in the bakery, so it's not ALL bad -- but . . .
>
> Does anybody have a room I can rent with my sweet little old dog?
>
> I gave up my long-term apartment on Circuit & Pennacook and, even though I thought I could beat the Vineyard Shuffle, I've now had two rentals fall through (note to self: get some therapy to figure out why I'm the island outcast. Or is it the village idiot?).

-- I've got cash on the barrelhead, although not summer visitor cash, more like modest islander cash.

-- As an animal lover, I'd be happy to feed and cuddle all manner of pets whenever you're away.

-- I can prepare a sweet vegetarian dinner for you on my half-day off (Sunday).

Would I get any leads? Could Facebook save a Vineyarder from seasonal homelessness? Or even—holy schlamoly!—permanent homelessness?

Homeless, *moi*? A daughter of the upper-middle classes? UCLA grad, member of the Writers Guild since, let's see, 19-fucking-70 - ?!

Stay tuned.

4

Glamping

I've been saved. My new rental will work if I can commit myself to "glamping." You know that word, don't you? It's a mashup of glamor and camping.

The glamor part is palpable. I have never dwelt within four more adorable walls. You know all those fantastic tiny houses we see taking up pages in style magazines? This one, my new home, is small, certainly, but not teeny tiny.

I once wrote a newspaper story about those teeny tiny cottages that you can stow on the back of a pickup truck. I had to ask the owner to please wait outside while I checked out the downstairs kitchen and living space about the size of a walk-in closet.

Upstairs was a loft for a single occupant or a single-occupant-with-guest when the guest would be leaving within the hour. I asked the fellow to step outside because claustrophobia was setting in, with two of us jostling for elbow room. Even my dog would have presented a claustro-aspect, and he only weighs thirty-three pounds.

So this backyard cottage I'm now renting measures 14 x 16. This appeals to me because I'm a diehard Thoreauvian in my quest to continue to carve out a life on an island that now rejects poor people.

Henry David's cabin famously measured 15 x 10 feet.

Sufficient for Henry, maybe sufficiant for me.

The ab fab part is that the woman who built this shelter herself, an autodidact carpenter, cute, petite lesbian named Bobbi, went a little nuts with the Cinderella effect, raising the roofline to a steeple, allowing for two loft spaces on either side of the interior, with skylights and mullion windows all around to catch the changing light in a rural part of town.

A vast skylight over my own head at night allows me vistas of the moon and, on darker nights, an overlook of our cousin stars I haven't seen since I last visited the Griffith Park Observatory. In grammar school.

And did I mention the walls, high ceilings, wooden subflooring, and ladder up to my sleep loft are ALL painted lavender? EVERY BIT OF IT! Lavender, oh lavender! The second favorite color of my childhood!

As I mentioned, my sister got pink. That's all the glam part.

The camping is a little tricky for this Valley girl who's been accustomed to creature comforts for much of her life. On the other hand, in my growing up years, my family camped at Yosemite. We pitched tents and cooked Spaghettios over open fires.

Also as a kid I happily trekked into the wilderness in the Big Bear Mountains with the Girl Scouts. I learned to chop wood and pack donkeys.

(Frankly, for the wood-chopping part, well, I'm fond of *Presto-Logs*. And donkey packing? Hasn't come up. But I could do it if you held a gun to my head. Or the donkey's head.)

So here's where camping enters the summer of 2018 in my life in my princess bower:

There's no plumbing.

No water hookup. At all.

A little off-shoot of a room, also graced with skylights and high windows, yields acomposting toilet. It's pretty basic. Under an ordinary ledge and toilet seat, the operation opens up to a metal pitcher with water which allows nitrogen to mix in an equation that's terrific for flowers.

Behind the pitcher stands a plastic bucket and wood shavings for optimum biodegrading.

This indoor/outdoor john calls for a biweekly carry out where the pitcher exits one door to enrich the rhododendron—and it really does; you get to see, over the weeks, the Miracle Gro effect of your pee+water on the flowers!—and the plastic bucket is removed through a trapdoor that flaps open like a baby's pajamas to accompany whatever composting materials are piling up in a stockaded plot.

Nuff said?

Maybe not. Because that marvel we all take for granted, conventional plumbing, implies a sink with a faucet, a bathtub, and all that good stuff for keeping cleanliness and Godliness intact.

My Cinderella cottage has none of that.

The wave of a Fairy Godmother's hand is very much missing.

So here's what I and my friend and landlady, Bobbi, have devised: A long shallow sink sans water pipe rests under a lovely long bank of paned windows. A beautiful ceramic tank beneath a *Poland* water-cooler jug hunkers over the sink.

I fill the three-gallon jug twice daily from the lower faucet of an outdoor shower. Yes! I've been jonesing for an outdoor shower during the long eight years I've lived in my previous apartment, which just goes to show for the millionth time be careful what you wish for: I got my outdoor shower but lost all access to indoor plumbing.

All I need to do when I wash my hands, or rinse a dish, or fill a tea kettle, is to switch on the water-cooler spigot. The water dribbles into the old sink, which itself looks like something the 49-ers used to pan gold, and falls into an opening which in most circumstances would shuttle through a pipe and be carried out to sea.

In my cottage this out-flow rustles into another plastic bucket which this pioneering woman, with a flair for interior decor, has encased in a gorgeous old wooden hatbox. And—TA DAH!—this hatbox is pink!

I empty it into the bushes each day.

Henry David would find the Cinderella part a bit *de trop*. But I think he'd chuckle at how much it mimics his own model cabin beside Walden Pond.

Funny, isn't it? that his memoir of life in the woods never refers to toilet needs. He must've tucked into the underbrush whenever Nature called. Oooh! And think of all those beans he raised.

Or don't!

We're in lockstep, Henry and I, and I'll let you know how we're getting on. Yeah, I know, as much as I'm floating him as if he's my sweetie, he was rumored to be gay, although antiseptically gay, maybe a lifelong virgin, but what does this matter with a cultural icon who's been dead for over 150 years?

Don't worry about my romantic life or my psychological health. God is my boyfriend.

Are we good now?

5

Back to the Laundromat

For all my newfound joy—and I use that word "joy" at the end of an ironical tweezers—at my vagabond life, I'm hit with a basic human situation that casts me into a considerable funk. Yes, as I cope with the gritty reality of a composting toilet, and a temporary stay from homelessness with this celestial cottage, I'm now up against the stark reality of dirty clothes.

I've left most of my wardrobe in the upstairs closet of the amiga who revoked my second rental.

That was her kind consolation prize: "Don't worry about your clothes. Come collect them when you're able."

We hardly need big wardrobes. I get comfortable with a few key items, in the summer a half-dozen sundresses made of cotton and some heavenly soft synthetic threads thrown in because, face it!, all the chi-chi organic threads—cotton, linen, and wool—are itchy as hell if not ameliorated with, I dunno, rayon? Polyester?

Minkledinklefolenfiber?

Now, most women do admittedly collect outfits stretching into untold garment racks if all were hung up, which they rarely are, unless you're one of those Hollywood wives with a full floor of mall-sized manors given over to closet space, curated by live-in staff. I recall from my Hollywood days that Candy Spellman, high on a plateau in Bel Air, had some six thousand square feet of wardrobe containment alone.

Dudes never get this need to buy one budget-popping outfit after another. I remember my beloved ex-husband Marty—when he was my future beloved ex—used to be amazed that I purchased the same straw hat over and over again.

I could see a resemblance, but each hat had its own distinct charm and advantage.

I believe we femmes acquire a new ensemble because the first time we wear it we feel like Audrey Hepburn waltzing with Cary Grant in *Roman Holiday*.

It's a remarkable high. Like the first quaalude, and all first samples of champagne or codeine; that first time is never to be duplicated, no matter how many second or hundredth tastes goes into reproducing the first.

Speaking of Audrey Hepburn, I recently came across this quote of hers: "I believe in **pink!**—I believe that laughing is the best calorie burner. I believe in kissing, kissing a lot. I believe in being strong even when everything seems to be going wrong. I believe that happy girls are the prettiest! I believe that tomorrow is another day and, I believe in miracles—"

Sorry! Just had to put this somewhere in the mix!

I too believe in pink! To *believe* in something makes it more than a color. It's a cause.

But where were we? . . . The best system for dealing with an excess of clothes wasformulated in Lee Child's Jack Reacher thrillers. Reacher, warrior of staggering ability, ex-military cop, and hobo extraordinaire, roams the American countryside with no i.d. to tie him to any old affiliations, no car, and no clothes other than what he sports on his brawny back. Every few days, as he saves a small town from a new crew of psychotic assholes, as he slip-slides through mud with a hailstorm of bullets firing all around him, when a change of clothes translates into a kindness to anyone with whom he comes into contact, he marches into an Army and Navy Store, or a small-town Sear's, and purchases a fresh outfit.

Briefs, sweatshirt, socks, tee-shirt, watch cap.

An undue expense? Reacher justifies it to anyone who asks, toting up what a mortgage on a house would cost, insurance, upkeep, and the utility bills to operate a washer and dryer. If we all lived his way, he argues, we'd save thousands of dollars a day.

A sword-tilt against bourgeois standards and climate change? You bet!

If nothing else, Jack Reacher is the ultimate modern-day Thoreau. A Thoreau who can rack, load, and shoot an AK-47.

So how dare I equate my homelessness with that of the American samurai Jack Reacher? Well, I could use his frugality program: here I am with three bulging canvas bags of dirty clothes, on my way down to the laundromat on the harbor.

My last ill-fated brush with this very laundromat occurred on December 24, 2010. My third husband Jack and I had frothed up a Keats-ian romance in the spring of 2009 in my borrowed digs in pastoral Chilmark.

Backstory: I'd lost all my money on a bookstore—Sun Porch Books 2002–2008 on the commercial strip of Oak Bluffs.

Post-bookstore crash, I lived in the enchanted art studio of my late great friend Dawn Greeley, on nine acres of Chilmark land off Old Ridge Hill Road, shrouded by blueberry fields and trees so dense that I named them after Winnie the Pooh's Hundred Acre Wood.

Nine years of celibacy had followed twenty-five years of marriage to beloved ex Marty, but then it yielded to erotic surrender to this gent Jack, bald, short, Irish, blue-eyed, wicked funny, with a high testosterone count (or so one would imagine), a book-a-day reading habit, and a reporting gig at the other island paper.

God knows why these things happen. Our attraction was so deep, I might even say severe, that Jack proposed to me within the first week of our dating.

I didn't wish to marry. Why would I?

I doubt he did either, in his heart of hearts. But I said "yes!" out of the sheer romance of it.

This proposal took place in his old truck after he drove me home from a play reading at the UU Church. It was Sinclair Lewis's *This Could Happen Here*.

We parked under the pale globe below my studio in Chilmark.

To stage-set his offer, he turned on the glaucous green overhead light in his truck that no woman, not even a twenty-two-year-old version of Gwyneth Paltrow, would want shining down on her face. I braved the glare through the quick, "Will you marry me?"

I squeaked, "Yes!" followed by, "Can you turn off the light now?!"

We wed in late October of 2009 in a potluck ceremony at the Aquinnah Town Hall, for the use of which we paid $25. Most of the guests were Jack's buddies in AA, so we clean forget about booze, although friends of mine provided wine, provoking them to spend half an hour scavenging in the kitchen for a bottle opener.

Our marriage proved as ramshackle as the cobbled-together wedding.

We were insanely incompatible. The romance was kaput directly after the wedding. We forgot how to seduce each other when we shared a futon pull-out bed. See, all along, in my Chilmark aerie, we'd shared a daybed too narrow for us to actually sleep together. Do you grok the rapture-making dynamic here?!

He had to go home every night! A bliss-out bonanza!

After marriage, we spent the summer of 2010 in Paris, figuring—rightly—we'd find cheaper lodgings in the City of Lights for the high season than we would on Martha's Vineyard. We leased a starving artist's flat for $700 a month, in a darling building off the Rue de Peronnet, a block north of the Cafe Flore and all the nifty shops of the Boulevard St. Germaine.

We even had Huxley with us! Dear old Hux, who was young at the time and prone to jump on all the white fluffy dogs whose elderly mistresses told us to keep him leashed.

"Il est trop fort!" they scolded. He's too strong.

For all the great lovers who've burned up the sheets and even cemetery plots of Paris, Jack and I made love one single time, in the flat bright light of one o'clock in the afternoon, and he upbraided me for being too voluble. The workmen—as the scion of the working classes in South Boston, Jack felt deep affiliation with them—the workmen in the flat below would hear me, he said with a snarl.

Elle est trop bruyant!

Was he kidding? This was Paris! At one in the afternoon, a perfect post-prandial hour, French workmen would be delighted to hear a woman's erotic moans in the apartment above them!

One can almost imagine caps swept from rumpled hair, then brandished to their hearts, *la Marseillaise* on their lips.

So now, our sad denouement at the laundromat in Oak Bluffs.

6

Laundromat, Deux

The laundromat down on the docks is a cheerful space. Or it should be. I realize now, looking back, that my spoiled Valley G tendencies jinxed the experience for me. From the sands of Malibu to the manifold owned homes and rentals on Martha's Vineyard, by the unfathomable decree of karma, I'd enjoyed washer-dryer sets to my heart's content, even though, like Marie Antoinette with her white-and-pink-and-gold layers of cake, I noticed not one whit how fortunate I was.

Until I had to learn to turn dollars to quarters to ply the machines down at the laundromat at the OB docks.

And then there was the Christmas eve visit when I lost it.

◆ ◆ ◆

Back up a few beats. Jack and I, post-Paris, "won" a year-round apartment in Oak Bluffs with the Affordable Housing crew. By the time we took possession, in September of 2010, of the spanking new second-floor apartment, carved out of the old OB library, our marriage was an old skiff sprung from a sinking ship, the skiff itself oozing water from a dozen bilge pumps. At last in late November we had one of those tired and trite conversations in which both of us, in croaking voices of failure, sued for a truce that would let each of us bolt.

Safely away from each other. Forevermore.

As the raven quothed.

So the plan was for me to keep the apartment. Jack would look around for his next billet. He accepted a good friend's offer of a cottage near the pastoral fields of Morning Glory Farm in Edgartown.

He moved out five days before Christmas.

I don't think either of us realized that this breakup crashing down on the holidays would have any ill effect. I know I didn't, until I threw all my dirty laundry into canvas sacks and hauled them down the long commercial block to the laundromat.

The date was late afternoon December 24.

I switched dollars for quarters and quarters for laundry soap and two washing machines' worth of sudsing. From overhead speakers, Christmas tunes chirped out. A flourish of trumpets for "Joy to the World." A sincere church choir for "Silent Night."

You know the playbill.

We've been subjected to that cheesy fare all our lives.

I started to hiccup. And hyperventilate. And cry. Well, I cried a little. A few tears, the kind we can wipe away with the back of our wrist. As I've said before, weeping is a lost art.

But I was seriously sad, alone in the laundromat, feeling no pleasure in the fact that this horrid jamboree of Christmas music was apparently aimed at me from a wisecracking universe.

I flipped open my phone and tottered outside to call Jack. For this early period of our disengagement, we held on to a tacit treaty that we were both still there for each other. Or at least I did. When he picked up—something he would be loathe to do in the near future—I told him about the dirty laundry and the canned Christmas music.

He walloped with laughter, the kind of laughter that had stirred my soul in the beginning months of our courtship, but that now had a nasty twang. At last he said: "Of course you feel crappy! Who spends Christmas eve at the laundromat?!"

◆ ◆ ◆

By the following spring, I made an arrangement with the

formidably wonderful Amy at Cottage City Appliances to pay cash outright for a washing machine, plus she allowed me to purchase, simultaneously, a dryer on the installment plan.

You've never seen a prouder w/d owner. When friends visited, I escorted them down the two steps to my spacious bedroom. I folded back accordion doors to the utility closet and, with the pure gloat of a Columbian cartel lord showing off his Duzenburgs and Bentleys in a glittering garage, I displayed my new appliances.

"Whaddya think?!"

♦ ♦ ♦

Fast forward to the spring of 2018, the advent of my hobo adventures, when a half-depleted wardrobe of dirty clothes led me back to that sad—for me—wash 'n dry joint down on the docks.

7

Laundromat, Trois

The price of a single wash had jumped from two bucks' of quarters to, yikes! thirty quarters. These thirty pieces of silver are, first, garnered from a cash machine into which one feeds umpteen neatly folded-and-hand-ironed-with-one's-palms-dollars, then lined up like little silver soldiers in the washing machine doohickey, *bam! blam! push!* until the requisite $12 for the cleansing has been, however ploddingly, obtained.

Wouldn't it be easier to wash my clothes by *WHAP! SLAP! KAPLOWING* them on boulders along a creek bed?

Like all broke and potentially homeless schlamozzles, I would prefer to do this endless operation of quarters and long waits as clothes flipped and flopped behind glass windows of dryers, but I have a serious time crunch.

I suddenly have a job.

This is something I've been spared in all my years on this planet of 7 billion working stiffs. The closest I've come was eleven years of independent contracting as a real estate agent on Martha's Vineyard, but the cool thing about that is you get to totally claim your own hours. Oh, you have your Up time when you'll gladly hold down the four-or-so hours as leads come churning in. For the remainder of the workday, you can breakfast with a pal in the morning, hike with the dog in the hills, fall onto your living room sofa for a long winter's nap and, if you've missed some office time, bop in around 8 p.m. and leave at midnight if you get that second wind.

But this new endeavor at the old Book Barn* has begun, something that turns out to be more fearful than my trepidation about homelessness, and this eats up a number of hours a day, seven days a week, plus it devours all my focus and eventually makes me acutely mentally ill, sucking all *joie de vivre* from my marrow and—hold on a sec!—I'm on my way to finishing up a lament about laundromats.

I hire a beautiful sweet Brazilian woman named Eleni to do my wash. For the fees I pay her, I could afford a whole new outfit, à la Jack Reacher, but she eliminates the possibility of me having to spend an evening a week at the place where I'd shed tears over Christmas carols.

So now on to the tale of the old emporium of used and rare books. Does it sound as if anything untoward can happen there?

Like something out of a Stephen King novel? I know, right?

8

The Scary-Ass Bookstore

Last September my friend Gwyn McAllister and I drove up New York Avenue out of town in her old beat-up blue Corolla; it looked great when she inherited it from her dad a few years before, but a phantom dumpster had come during the night and poured in a shitload of trash.

Now both our dogs were in the back seat with most of the junk, my Huxley and her Felix, who looks like a werewolf puppy, with wild bulging black eyes and an overbite long past salvation by braces.

Over on the right we saw a sign outside the iconic Book Barn: *CLOSING FOR THE SEASON TODAY, 50% OFF ALL BOOKS.*

Gwyn, nineteen years younger than I, rail thin with chop-cut blond hair and black-rimmed hipster glasses, is a mad reader and an obsessional bargain hunter, of equal proportions.

She hung a U-ey with a theatrical peel of rubber and, seconds later, we poured through the front room of books in the two-story musty, moldy barn, in business, according to a plaque over the door, since 1976.

On top of so many other talents of Gwyn's, she can shop with the directness and dexterity of a chipmunk on Adderall. Within minutes she had a pile of reads for herself, about seven books high, mostly true crime nonfiction, and another for me of equal height. And I knew before looking that all her choices for me—eclectic; hard-boiled mysteries, something by Margaret Drabble, a big ol' tome about Catherine the Great of Russia—would be spot on!

I didn't even see him at first, Dimitri*, a seventy-five-ish man with diminishing pale hair and a rotund, pinky face, spoke from a low chair set some feet back from the counter, and even well below the counter, as if he'd found a place to nap without anyone noticing.

"Say, Holly, why don't you buy this store?"

I slapped my hand on my pile of reading material. "I'm not even sure I can buy these books!"

He chuckled. At this early stage of our dealings, he was determinedly agreeable.

"You know we were discussing you the other day? Zoya* and I are overjoyed to live on our contry estate in Belarus, so we need someone who knows books to sell books, and here you've had your own store. How would you like to run the Book Barn next summer? We could have some kind of profit-sharing. Say 50/50?"

A handsome proposition, but I took none of this seriously. I have no capacity to make plans for the distant haul, the distant haul in this scenario being nine months away the following June.

Oh, I love to fantasize clear into coming eons: "I plan on living in Sicily in my sunset years. Unless the apartment with Elderly Housing comes through before then."

Just kidding: Elderly Housing would need to pry Sicily from my cold dead hands.

And I had no need of a job per se. We live in a money-grubbing society but, call me crazy, I have little urge to grub myself, just so long as I have enough bucks to get by. My enough may not be your enough; in fact, I'm sure it's not.

I have a Writers Guild pension that's about one millionth of Steven Bochco's, and a Social Security payment that could provide for the feeding of a single meerkat in a desert zoo but, so far, when I factor in the monthly monies for my freelance articles for the local paper, and modest residuals for the six books I've written, five of which are still in print, I do a'ight.

On the Tuesday before the Wednesday when my Social drops into my checking account, I might be squeezing my eyes shut, praying for nothing to bounce, but overall, it's okay. I'm okay.

But here's the tragic short-sightedness of this mentality: Standing by the counter of the Book Barn in September of 2017, I had no idea how Martha's Vineyard, by the spring of 2018, would finally be out of reach of us po' folk. As the venerable saying goes, "If you have to ask the price, you can't afford it."

Don't ask the price of *ANYTHING* on MV.

This man sitting below the counter gave me his contact info by way of a brochure for his country estate in Belarus, log cabins on a great whacking amount of acres, that took in guests. I pocketed it in such a way that it ended up in a drawer that I pulled out many months hence at a time when I believed it could do me some good. Not because of the profit sharing, although I ended up needing it: the scary bookstore cost me a lot of loot.

Excuse me while I go pop a couple of *gabapentins*. My long-term use—and consequent addiction to—*gabapentin* has ended up, ickily enough, having much to do with this story.

And the tabs are orange; you'd think while they're at it the lab could pop out some in pink.

9

My Own Wee Depression and Other Gossipy Bio Bits

Oops, got carried away there. Permit me a brief flashback.

Back up a couple of months, it is in fact April and I'm again on Martha's Vineyard, in my darling two-room apartment in the old library of Oak Bluffs, and I have no intention of staying here; in fact, I've given notice to be out at the end of May.

Whereupon my two failed rentals will occur but I don't know that yet.

I exchange emails with Dimitri in Belarus and he and his wife Zoya are pleased to have me run the store.

"You'll be perfect for this!" he exults. We're now closing in on his final exultation before he turns mean.

He's right to exult over me! I love books and book chat and book lovers and my commitment to run the Book Barn looms as the one positive thing that's happened to me this year. Or ever!

But there's so much to take care of, I can barely breathe.

Interiors. Interiors have always had a lot to do with my life, and my way of same. I wonder if that's why I bounce around so much, to create fresh backdrops: white plasterboard crying out for a few coats of semi-gloss raspberry paint?

Back in California in January when my mom and sister and I played at being the new Golden Girls, I fixed up my dad's old study into a classy bedroom replete with a gilded mirror and elegant rocking chair retrieved from the garage, and originally acquired from an antiques dealer on the Vineyard.

My sister decided her later hours from work dictated I cede this dining-room-adjacent chamber to her, so I proceeded to redo the large back forty of a bedroom with views of the mountains. I accented the aged gold glint of the wallpaper with gold and white textiles, pushed the double bed back against the corner for a cozy nook, and removed years of sororal hoarding to freshen the overall setting.

My sister took umbrage at my abrupt treatment of her stuff—I'd piled it up in a corner of the living room—and this plus another one thousand imagined injustices launched the fights that drove me back to the east coast.

I have a knack for decorating. But how many times can one scramble a new beautifully accessorized abode inside of two weeks? On the island, and with Leigh's help and his old white truck, I carried away from my apartment the last of my desirable items to that bum boardinghouse of a rental. When that went belly-up, as mentioned, I stocked everything in the front room of the bookstore. Now why would I do this without notifying the bloke in Belarus?

You might think me a crafty dealer who could do whatever she wants with this business some 7,000 miles away from its owner, the East Euro country squire. But here's the rub: I thought I was—and appeared to be—completely on my own.

A lovely and well-preserved Victorian manse sits in front of the bookstore. And surprise! surprise! the Belarusian dude's son* lives here, a big blocky dark-haired boy in his forties, a police officer in the adjacent village of Edgartown.

When I first ask for a look-see of the barn, dad tells me his son would give me a tour. A son, huh? That would come in handy.

On the day I cycle over, I'm met by the son's mother-in-law. Nice lady, real estate agent, bouffant silver hair. But *tant pis*, both her daughter and the cop are down with a tummy bug. As the days wear on, the son answers none of my emails, most of them along the lines of "how are you feeling?"

It dawns on me that neither he nor his young wife want anything to do with me or the venerable bookstore.

I misdiagnose this as indifference rather than a territorial surge of epic and phobic proportions, played out by blocking me at every turn so I'd be bound to screw up, but I'm left with a sense that no one *in situ* cares about the booky bidness; if I were to leave my domestic belongings in the front room until I fly back out west to pick up my dog before my agreed-upon start date of June 1, who is there to care or to mind?

I would soon find out.

But hang on! At the top of this chapter I promised you a fun and breezy breakdown of my depression and, instead, detoured to the missing cop son and daughter-in-law in the big house facing the road, and all my junk crammed into the front room of the Book Barn.

So let us blaze on to that quibbling matter of a mood-that-often-sucks and the medication that keeps it at bay.

10

Sucky Moods

It's the first harsh email from Dimitri the Belarusian dude and, while it bums me out to a considerable degree, I roll up my socks and deal with it. All would be, could be, explained.

He writes, "I need you to know I *HATE* surprises. Every plan of yours, every little change, must be reconciled with me. *DO YOU UNDERSTAND THIS?!* My son informs me you've crammed a whole household of furniture and every other damn thing into the bookstore and this is shocking. *SHOCKING!* What were you thinking?! Are you planning to *LIVE THERE OR RENT OUT SLEEPING SPACE?!* Now hear this: get rid of all your belongings *N-O-W!*"

Looking back, I should have seen the signs of inherent meanness and madness, and walked away, *das vidaniya*. But I also realized how odd it looked, me having off-loaded a ton of personal effects into his store. I seek to explain to him:

"Dimitri, I didn't want to bog you down with my own hassles." And then I lay it out, as cleanly as possible, the cashiered year-round apartment, the two failed rental prospects, and salvation in the form of the Glamp Cottage which would be ready for tenancy on June 1, after I return from California.

I outline my plans to once again hire Leigh as I set up the bookstore and redirect the goods.

"And, Dimitri, the silver lining of me having to move, as far as the Book Barn is concerned, is that I've got stuff to bestow on the property: Chairs, a couple of wicker sofas for the garden, lamps to light up some of the shadowy spaces. Upstairs—perhaps your son and daughter-in-law have told you—I've organized a salon area where we can hold book clubs and authors' events and other kinds of lectures."

Dimitri fires back: "We've had a couple of salon events in the past, spent a lot of money on cocktails, and made nothing on book sales."

Me: "That's mystifying, Dimitri. From my own experience, when you round up book lovers, they buy books. They fling them into sacks and pack them in their hatch-back trunks. You somehow missed the boat on that one. A very reliable old tug of a boat."

We go back and forth, with the Belarusian squire asking distrustful questions, and me having to defend *this* position and *that* choice. Finally, around 11 at night, my time in California, when it would have been 5 p.m. and three days hence in Belarus, I type, "I'm tired. I'm discouraged. Whatever qualities you thought I could bring for the benefit of the shop, I still have those qualities. Do you want me or don't you?"

"We want you."

♦ ♦ ♦

Had I known this affiliation with the bookstore and the final ferocious tug to carve a living out of Martha's Vineyard in the summer of 2018 would cost me my last shard of happiness, I would have backed away at this bewildering juncture. But how much prescience do we possess in our own private lives? Seems we only have hindsight, which, I imagine, we try to hoover up for its meaning to protect us the next time prescience is called for.

Whoops! Once again I've missed my chance to fill you in, darling reader, on my depression *problemo*, so let's just pass that along for another, more congenial time.

Should one of those arise.

11

Starting Over

Before I return to Martha's Vineyard, Dimitri tells me that his son Boroda* and daughter-in-law Tami* will be working the Barn over Memorial Day weekend, so it's incumbent on me to "get rid of your junk. All of it! NOW!"

Because I'm still strangely willing to make the best of things, thinking my summer roll-out of the legendary old bookstore will be life-changing, I call good ol' boy Tripp Barnes, owner of Barnes Moving, and arrange for a couple of his lads to come, pick up my stuff, store it for a couple of weeks, then haul it to my Cinderella cottage.

"And, please, Dimitri," I email the Belarusian squire, "can you make sure Boroda and Tami leave the circle of chairs and sofas upstairs? I'm committed to hosting book club and authors' events."

He sends me a c.c. he's shipped to son, *"Leave chairs upstairs."*

◆ ◆ ◆

When I return to the island, my first sight of the Book Barn's front parlor is a total shocker.

Everything of my own is gone.

Even those objects that should have been obvious were placed there for an upgrade, such as pens in a ceramic jar, a giant stapler, a blue-and-yellow ceramic tissue holder, and the lamp on the front counter, a long-necked bulb thrust through the base of an ancient Roman urn that my dad and I excavated in 1960 from a 2,000-year-old municipal dump—archeologists of the time had offered the refuse pile to whomever might want a lark of digging shit up—this inestimably valuable lamp had been banished from the Barn into the moving truck, along with wooden book displays retained from Sun Porch Books, and small square stained-glass panels for the windows.

It's the Insult Direct, a clear-cut message of, "We want *NOTHING* to do with you! You're a species of E.coli we're hoping to obliterate with a tub of Cipro." Upstairs, shiver me timbers, the salon of wicker furniture is gone.

You know what? Thanks to the Belarus Eastern European ancestry and a consonant-ridden last name for this pops-and-son team, their joint maneuvering reminds me of Stasi agents in Cold War East Berlin. Call me crazy, but I hate the idea of Stasi agents crawling through my life.

Well, that's it. I click my dog back on his leash, don my denim jacket, throw my pink floral backpack over my shoulder, and head for the front house.

I'm quitting.

At the same time I'm thankful for the early warning of doom and general unfixable fuckupedness.

If only I'd paid attention to this blinking red light. You know the one: that blinking light in Disneyland's Mr. Toad's Wild Ride, with the sign above the black cave that reads "*GO BACK! GO BACK!*", a warning the roadster ignores, only to blast through a barrier, as it plunges into cavern dankness.

And a last thought about the dank cavern: My bill from Barnes Moving for collecting my stuff, storing it for a couple weeks, and redelivering to my new rental: "3,554.95."

The proceeds from Boroda and Tami's Memorial Day weekend—as I later glean from the sales log—$245.

12

I'm Outta Here and I'm Sorry It Took So Long

It's a Saturday morning when Boroda, Edgartown cop, and Tami, accountant at an Oak Bluffs bank, are home. I knock on the door. Tami opens. She's blond and pretty without conceit, always cordial, an all-around nice person.

A couple of times she's come over to consult with me on bookstore operations and we've enjoyed intimate chats, as if I'm her auntie Holly. Afterward she's left me little gifts on the bookstore counter, a vintage milk bottle filled with hydrangeas, a fresh notebook with a Japanese etching of a schoolgirl on the cover.

I say, "Can I talk to the two of you?"

Seconds later I stand in their kitchen, a square sunny place with central granite counters and no warmth, not a pair of quilted pot holders, nor a pastel valance on the windows over the sink. The fridge holds an 11 x 17 color photograph of the newlyweds with their heads tipped together. She's smiling, he's expressionless, but I study his blue eyes to see if there's a sparkle within.

Doesn't seem to be.

Are those eyes lonely, forlorn, longing for love?

More likely he's wondering where he stashed his pepper spray and handcuffs.

But the live customer himself stands behind the granite. Tami offers me a croissant: "I just made them from scratch!"

Under normal circumstances who wouldn't want a homemade croissant fresh from the oven? But these aren't normal circs.

"No, thank you. I've come to say I can't do this job at the bookstore. I think you, Boroda, could have hurt the feelings of Joseph Goebbels, but it takes far less of an assault with me. I happen to be on the sensitive side. Truth be told, and I see no reason you deserve the truth, but I'm probably too sensitive to live, and your treatment of me—the removal of every last paper clip of my own from the bookstore, was deplorable. Tell your pops I'm out of here! Happily out of here!"

They're contrite, or at least Tami is contrite.

And because he stands beside her, Boroda could pass for contrite at a two-degree remove.

They argue for a second chance.

We talk about strategies for working together. They suggest a walk-through of the upstairs part of the barn to find a suitable place for a circle of chairs and sofas, explaining that my own central location had raised concerns for them about people tripping over things. Instead they offer a partitioned area currently housing Dimitri's wife's art for sale.

"But won't she mind?" I ask.

Boroda almost smiles. I can actually see an isometric push-pull of the muscles around his mouth. Okay, he dislikes his stepmother. Obviously anything impinging on the family brand will engage his passion to suppress, repress, and oppress. Have I left any resses out?

At the end of an hour, I'm thinking the three of us are completely in accord. As an addendum, but an important one, I raise the issue of bathroom privileges. Yes, it's true what Tami's mother had originally explained to me: I could use the loo off the kitchen, but no one else could ever piggy-back this executive pass.

Boroda tells me this with a narrowing of his already fiercely hostile Stasi eyes that make me wonder if he's even deadlier than he seems. Could someone borrow my key to their kitchen back door, use the toilet, and end up with a Soviet-era military cloak thrown over their head, after which he or she would be carted to the patch of soil behind the barn and buried in the black oily soil?

For my full time of using the kitchen loo at the couple's house, I would pass the photo of the newlyweds and ask myself again and again: Those eyes—did a drop of humanity reveal itself in the inchoate irises? I never detect any, but it doesn't mean none existed.

Maybe he really *is* lonely and forlorn.

One last cop-ish incident occurs that day.

Before I leave, Boroda says, "You know that guy you use to move stuff?"

I nod. How would he know about Leigh? Boroda is always away during the day. Isn't he? He says, "He has a criminal record. I need you to keep him off the property."

I inwardly groan. Poor Leigh. My new best amigo. And, again, how does this unfriendly brute know my sad sack of a townie helper has been on the scene, and how has he scarfed up his felony record? Can you do that? Even a cop?

13

It Ain't All Bad . . . Is It?

You know what I miss? The diagnosis of manic depression. Manic depression for everyone!

Ya want some? We're all on that spectrum! As the addicts used to say on *The Wire*, can you feel me?

It's the human condition!

Who can understand this bipolar business?

Seems like a serious head-case kind of problem when you consider *A Beautiful Mind* with the math genius scribbling equations on the mirror of a public john. The bipolar tag features people who walk on overhead electric wires or run at a pasture of cows waving umbrellas.

They're *mishug*. The heart bleeds for them, but does it help people to receive this fearsome label? If we could all just default back to manic depression, we'd find it far, far easier to make our way in life.

Talk around the water cooler would go something like this:

"Didya have a good weekend?"

"Not so much. Too depressed to do anything but stare at Netflix."

"Maybe Netflix is causing the depression."

"Ya think?"

"Let's you and me go for a walk right now. I find fresh air is the cure for melancholy. As well as Wellbutrin, lithium, and CBD oil."

"That's some cocktail ya got there."

"We all need a cocktail. But it takes years to find out what works."

You know what else helps? The color pink! Makes us feel good! They've done studies. If you can count ten pink items, your mood lifts as you finish the list!

> *pink ballet slippers*
> *pink dahlias*
> *pink eyeglasses such as the pair Randy Rainbow*
> *sports after he's given DonaldTrump what-for*
> *pink baseball caps, no matter the team*

But getting back to manic depression, I pick my way along a primrose path of nearly constant sadsackishness as a kind of fallback, with bright lights throughout the day of laughter, shiny conversation—shiny if only because affection is freely exchanged, hugs, stupid animal tricks, even stupider human tricks, and more laughter.

For my melancholy, however, I take this weird-ass stuff called *gabapentin,* generic for Neurontin. It's a treatment for epilepsy, but a few years back researchers got wind of the fact that it helps some people—a relatively small percentage, more's the pity—to spin around in a mental *tour jeter* and feel better for hours.

And did I receive this news from my longtime shrink, Dr., um, let's think of a good cover name, Dr. Weinberger*? Yes, of course he's Jewish, have you ever met a full MD-certified-psychiatrist who wasn't?!

But about his own creative impulse toward prescribing, naw. The only time his lightbulb went off regarding the right medication for me was when I'd first consulted him at his office across the bay in Falmouth. It was September of 2000. My dad had just died of a heart attack cum fall down the stairs, without the docs knowing if the heart attack had triggered the fall or vice versa. After that came a five-day coma at Lawrence Hospital north of Boston and then . . . flatline.

And yeah, I was in mourning, but it also occurred to me I'd been basically bummed all year, even during a two-week visit to my homegirl Kathy Q in Paris. Who gets depressed in Paris? Well, actually I do, but all the same, I recalled sitting in holy quiet at Kathy's parish cathedral Sainte-Clotilde. They were holding a month-long tribute to Therese of Lisieux, replete with cardboard cutouts of the fabulously pious young nun, the "little saint," and I sat in a front pew, weeping.

Just fucking weeping.

Who weeps in Paris parish cathedrals?—well, never mind, I do. I did. As mentioned, I, like most women over a certain age, don't cry anymore, or hardly ever.

So I asked Dr. Weinberger if he'd prescribe me an antidepressant. I thought I'd have to do a whole song and dance, ya know, prove my craziness, like the oral exam for your doctorate, with plenty of pointed questions.

He reached for his pad and said, "We might as well start you on the gold standard: Prozac."

It was my sister, a number of years later, who told me about the psychotropic benefits of *gabapentin*. She's a recreation therapist working in hospitals and she kitbitzes with the shrinks about all the new junk.

As I would if I had her access.

◆ ◆ ◆

Cut to me in the spring of 2010 in my doc's office asking if he'll let me try this new med; take it out for a test drive.

It was odd how he allowed me to order this up like eggs benedict, but he placed a call right there in his office that went something like this:

"Hi, it's me. What's the dosage for Neurontin?" He wrote it down. It was a helluva lot. Probably didn't look so bad on paper, but the pharmacy sent me home with two tall bottles of 240 tabs, 400 MG per, take two capsules four times a day.

I swallowed the first dose in April 2010. My third husband

Jack and I had found a cottage to rent along the farmland stretch Indian Hill Road in West Tisbury. We might have been happy there in a forever home kind of way—or at least until our marriage fell apart, which it was on the cusp of doing—but we had plans to scoot across the sea for a gay Paree summer.

In this wayside retreat, Jack kindly handed over full territorial control of an upstairs tower room, with windows facing all directions, and a black metal spiral staircase that required two full months for Huxley to dare to climb.

So I sat on the only furniture in the small tower, a double bed, just the box springs and mattress on the floor. Hux sprawled at my feet, as he always did—he had a security detail kind of fixation about his human and setting up a perimeter for me. In a previous life he must've been an Israeli *Mossad* agent.

So, I'd downed my first two 400 MG babies about an hour and a half before. I began my morning meditation, full breaths up to ten, then over again. For the first twenty minutes all was normal, dull, routine, and then at the pause at the top of the in-breath, the one that seems to colonize the crown of the head and, if you're paying real attention, the third eye with its Kriya blue light and the gold dot seen for a moment at the apex, time elongated.

It just stretched out like the lapping play of water flowing around a bend in the Tallahassee River.

Oh, I thought. So that's what this *gabby* stuff does. It relaxes you into the Eternal Now.

As if you're a luscious odalisque spread out on the *chaise lounge* of life.

That was the only high I experienced on that first course of *gabapentin*. I was to learn from hard experience that every time I gave up the drug, as one does for the sake of embracing what you convince yourself is mental health and physical well-being, the nasty med rolls you slowly down into the swamp of depression.

It takes a couple of weeks.

After a few times of bidding *gabby* farewell, it no longer plays games with you. It's a harsh bitch that dumps you right down into the dungeon of despair.

The kind of despair that makes you fantasize about hemlock,

or is there a high enough ridge with pointy rocks way down below to make your jump really count for something?

And here's what's fun.

After moving heaven and earth to get the motherfucker re-prescribed, that first "taste" is always . . . *MARVY*. It's the classic free ride from the Candyman Dealer: you're bound to love it and so you want more. And the more with *gabapentin* is nothing, only a reprieve from the dungeon.

There must be some way of taking it that provokes a continuing buzz. It's been stamped with some schedule or other, you know, the way heroin is Schedule 3? *Gabby's* not that extreme, but something about it has raised a DEA eyebrow. Sometimes this makes me ponder what you can do with this stuff to stir it into ambrosial action.

Do you cut it in lines with a razor as you would cocaine? Gulp a whole bunch?

Sauté it in coconut oil?

I'd come to rely on my *gabby* to rise and fight again another day. In that June of 2018, the Book Barn was off to a bumpy start with the Stasi boys, but otherwise I adored it! There was the upstairs travel section with such esoteric delights as Dame Freya Stark's adventures in the Middle East! During WWII the military relied on her for intel about the relatively unknown region. Downstairs sprawled the central stacks of paperback fiction, linking up to the surrounding three walls of hardback fiction!

The customers were a constant confection, about half of them lured by my Facebook posts. In the first week, a pair of male pilots arrived, in their forties, blond, handsome self-confident blokes, and we talked, what else? aviation. I showed them a first edition of Amelia Earhart's book, *The Last Voyage.*

"Do you see how ironic that is?" I cried. "How could she know it was her final flight?"

I explained to them she had originally titled her memoir, *Voyage around the World.* Then when she disappeared, her publishers thought an amended title was in order.

I pressed the pilots for their own close calls. This sparked them to memories of the night JFK Jr. splashed down in our own onyx-sparkling waters, only a few clicks from his mom's estate in Aquinnah.

I said, "Do you think there's some mother issue he should have pursued in therapy?"

The older one shook his head. "I think heading for home is a sign of looking for—and expecting—safety."

So you see how lovely June was turning out to be. Irresistible customers.

Purple wisteria wrapping around Victorian porches.

Baby lambs frisking in the fields. And don't eat those lambs! Promise?

14

Is Jupiter in Westchester?

When things get especially tense or *in*-tense or, not to put too fine a point on it, fucked-up-beyond-any-last-hope-of-even-the-most-modest-redemption, I turn to my brilliant friend Niki Patton, a thoroughly original astrologer. Also a singer, musician, and monologuist. I first caught her act—or part of her multifeatured act—during a winter's Chilmark Community Center talk on—my own title—New Wowie Zowie Alternative theories.

Niki started with: "I don't believe in astrology but . . . it works!"

I'm not sure I believe in it either, but when you're tied to train tracks and a butter-fingered railway bum is trying to free you, plus dark clouds have rolled low to spit snow in your face, it helps to learn that all of us are going through a similar seismic zodiacal shift before we make it to safety, reinvigorated, a cup of hot cocoa in our hands.

As we stood inside the shadowy front parlor of the Book Barn, Niki, statuesque like the Nike goddess statue in the foyer of the Louvre, with her mane of white hair falling to her waist, advised me:

"Mars turns retrograde on the twenty-first which will put a twang like an electric wire in all our dealings. Chiron is in Aries and Uranus in Taurus, which makes all human dealings tricky, but—and this is vital—starting on the thirteenth, Venus in Leo makes us more creative."

I don't know why but hanging these descriptive labels on everything relaxes me. In these first days, June blossoms like the white lotus it should be and often is.

Before I take up residence in the Cinderella cottage, I spend a couple of weeks in a favorite home-away-from-home (particularly apt when you have no set address), the Tivoli Inn on upper Circuit in Oak Bluffs. In the off season, chatelaine Lisa gives me, well first, an amazing discount, and the front-facing chamber on the second floor, with high ceilings and French doors opening to a porch that overlooks the park across the street.

And Huxley is welcome too!

Favors like these occur only when you've lived in Shangri La for a long, long time and Shangri La-ans take a shine to you.

Especially with Venus heading toward Leo. Or is it Leo heading toward Venus?

The Book Barn so far is fun, not yet LeCarré spy novel scary. I have two days to go at the Tivoli, and the only small concern is that I'm running out of *gabapentin.*

Normally my shrink and I play a game of Mexican standoff as I call in a possible script from Dr. Weinberger, check with the pharmacy, "Anything? No?" hating how clearly the drug store peeps pity me, then lighting up with joy and a transcendent feeling of being loved, loved the way I wish I'd been loved as an infant, when my medication is filled five minutes before closing time.

As part of the mental illness gavotte that we do, I ask the doc for an appointment to touch base. I make an effort to see him every other month, which costs me $150. I'm grandfathered in at that price. Seems shrink visits have shot up to $300 or more. So he'll accommodate me on Thursday 7:30 p.m. Kinda late, but if that's what's on the table, *on y mange.* The way we've both timed things, I've got enough *gabbies* to last me through the night. He'll hand me a new prescription and I'll fill it in the morning, first thing, 'cause you don't wanna start the sweaty labor of withdrawal.

I take a taxi.

It's worth it to haul all that way in the dark through the hinterlands of Vineyard Haven. I look forward to our usual way of killing the half hour. It's been years since he's attempted any kind of talk therapy, and sometimes I wonder if this is because he's ceased to admire me or even like me.

It feels that way.

In my bookstore days he used to call me a success. But then the store fell in the undertow of the Recession. I spent a year away from him until I moved to the Hundred Acre Wood in Chilmark, and deep depression gobbled me whole for a few weeks, this at a time when I stared out the windows of my aerie and thought:

"As soon as these blues fade away, I'm going to love it here!" And I was right!

The way my shrink and I spend our half hour is, believe it or not, sifting through the shrapnel and beads of iron and glass found in the sands of World War II.

I've got a sort of sore spot about the Holocaust, well, what Jew hasn't?

I didn't discover I was Jewish until the age of sixteen when my great-uncle Aaron, a chicken rancher in the hills above Santa Barbara—Aaron Goldberg, can you believe I didn't know from Jewish names?!—anyway, when one night we walked home from the hen barn under a lambent evening sky, he pointed a bony finger at me and decreed in that sort of pharisaical way ancient uncles have:

"You were born Jewish and your parents can't take that away from you!" Whoa-wait-what?!!

He was also an avid astrologer, something unusual, even unknown in the early '60s.

When I told this, decades later, to my beloved (future) ex-husband Marty, he said: "Soyou learned you were Aquarius with Jew Rising?"

Thing is, whenever I sink into real depression, I find myself treading over two events: The loss of our seaside cottage in East Chop and the extermination of 6 million Jews in Europe.

You might think I'm a total bimbo to position my own little piffled past against, arguably, history's greatest injustice, but there's no accounting for that old black magic of the broken psyche.

But on this night in early June 2018, this man, this psychiatrist, has it in for me.

15

Ambush by Shrink

I tell him, *naturellement* (he did his residency at the American Hospital in Paris, so we have Paris in common too), I need a refill on the *gabapentin*. Instead of the usual drill of pulling out his pad, he transfers to a kiddo-sized desk, hunkers over his computer, and pulls up a chart. This is beginning to feel sinister.

The doc makes me come over to view the data. It's my own past few many months' records of refills; of *gabapentin* but also the Xanax that I stopped taking last November.

He asks, "Did you know the government keeps track of your drug habits?"

Only mine?

"Uh no."

Indeed this is chilling. We're plunged into the harrowing movies the kids watch today with robots and mythological monsters and the big crimson eye of the mother ship scoping everything we do.

He tells me something I already know, that *gabapentin* has received some kind of "schedule." Not as bad as Hell-on-wheels opiates, but . . . he points to my chart. "Every month you've been filling the *gabapentin* a week ahead of time."

"Well, my insurance lets me do that, so I figure it's not a problem."

"It's a big problem for me," he says, his voice filled with a pharisaical thunder I've never heard before.

You'll note I've used "pharisaical" twice in a few pages, which may be some kind of world record.

I step backward and fall into my chair. My doc of nineteen years returns to the chair opposite me. He breathes stertorously through his nose and says, "I suggest you see Charlie Silverstein for your medications."

Silverstein is the single other year-round psychiatrist on the island. Back in the '90s when we lived on the shore and our social circle included, on occasion, the Styrons, Art Buchwald, and Carly Simon, I contacted Silverstein for my first run at antidepressants. He said he preferred not to mix social ties with doctor/patient business.

Of course now, a couple of decades later, with my ass having bumped down the chain of multiple status levels, I don't know if the shrink's shibboleth still applied, but it seemed to me that That Way Be Dragons.

I'm shocked.

My shrink is breaking up with me.

When I protest, his features set in a deep squint.

"*HAVE YOU EVER BEEN INVESTIGATED?!*" he roars, making me thump back in my seat.

An odd question. Almost laughable, although to laugh would have put me, I fear, in some kind of unknowable jeopardy. Still, I cock my head, consider his question, and ask meekly, "I'm a writer. What would I be investigated for? Bad grammar?"

But something else is bothering him. "You posted on Facebook a little story about getting off Xanax."

Gosh, so I had. How does he know this? We aren't Facebook friends, God forbid. And how does he know it? And why does it matter? My post had been jocular, a sort of casual lead at an AA meeting.

For years and years I'd been taking a single Xanax before bedtime. Crap! Could I sound any more pathetic? Up until now you might not have thought this possible. But wait! It *WAS* a funny story.

For the Thanksgiving of 2017, I'd taken a road trip with my

beloved ex-husband. We met in Boston at South Station, hailed the train to Hartford where Marty's cousin Linda picked us up for a preholiday few days in Armonk, a sweet rural village in Westchester; then a train ride or two down to Astoria to lodge in an AirBnB apartment near our son and daughter-in-law, followed by fun on the sacred T Day itself with Cary's gay uncles in the countryside that curves way above Brooklyn.

So I was back on the Vineyard, and I'd carefully conserved my last Xanax for that Sunday night, with a vital plan to call my shrink for a refill come Monday morning.

With the usual several calls to let him know the situation was dire.

♦ ♦ ♦

I stand over the sink, I oh so carefully open the bottle, maybe too carefully, because pop! it flipped out and up and spun a double axel before sliding with perfect precision down the drain.

I stared at the drain while I considered: Any way I could screw open the pipes and dig through the balls of hair and other gunk and find the precious yellow pill?

I was up until three in the morning.

No surprise there.

It's the insomniac's burden exacerbated by cold-cocking the Xanax.

The next day, as I wrote in my FB journal about this business, I consulted with the lovely pharmacist, short, kindly Paula with a pageboy of brown hair. I put it to her: Should I take advantage of this accidental shit-canning of the tranquilizer to go sober?

She encouraged me to try. She said *gabapentin* is useful for sleep, so I could rely on that alone.

So that's my quaint "little story."

I received a bunch of "likes." Of course! Everyone approves of laying off the drugs. Sometimes Facebook makes you feel like you've just delivered the best lead at an AA meeting.

But now my psychiatrist, many moons later, carries forward

a sense of injustice that I hadn't relied on him for any help, that I'd written up the account as if there was no wizard of a doctor watching over me.

I don't know where any of this is coming from. I still don't.

"You sound paranoid," I say at last, wondering how often in therapy the patient gets to bop the analyst in the head with a diagnosis.

He berates me some more for my commentary on Facebook. I lower my head, shake it despairingly. How is this happening? Already in this half-year I've been blasted by my sister in the California desert until I shuttled away in voluntary exile. I've given up my precious year-round rental on the island, only to be bitch-slapped by the NASCAR racer's brother who'd promised me a sunroom, and my friend who couldn't "be the one to rescue me."

What was it my pal Niki said about Mars turning retrograde and causing twangs like electrical charges in the human psyche?

But I never would have thought, I mean this with all my heart, I never would have thought my shrink of nearly two decades, who'd seen me through two divorces, a thriving then faltering bookstore, a son in college with his various girlfriends, his hero's journey to LA, then back east to New York, all of it, all of it, perhaps provoking the doc to strenuously disapprove of me.

"Do you—do you even like me anymore?" I ask. No, I don't ask. I squeak. I'm supremely curious. And hurt.

He stares at me. The blank stare that is the bane of my existence, from my mother's blank stare and lack of response and hugs and compliments, to the blank stares of all those dear conventional souls out there whom I've learned not to work too strenuously to charm.

He will prescribe the *gabapentin*, just not before its time, as Orson Welles used to say about the wine he pushed in commercials. So now I have five more days before the medication, by his measure, and that odd record on his laptop, could be refilled. He sends me away to a day of reckoning. And then four more days of reckoning in which I could very well be checked into the ER.

In the morning I lie on my bed at the cozy inn, depleted

like Clark Kent with a snootful of kryptonite. I have to open the bookstore, but . . . As the morning wears on, I sigh and reach over to the bed table that holds a lovely little hand-painted wooden tryptic of the Virgin Mary. I purchased it in Rome a few years ago on that narrow street that files forth from the Pantheon to the Piazza Navona.

I place the Blessed Mother on my chest over my heart. I whisper a prayer. The phone rings.

This is how the mystic's journey with its tiny miracles tends to operate. It's my shrink. There is no affect in his voice as he explains he's called in an emergency five days of *gabapentin* to take me up to the next "legal" refill which he has also re-upped. I'm overjoyed that he's making this effort to save me.

But what was that chamber of horrors in his office? I never call him again or see him again.

I would find other ways to come by my *gabbies*.

Does he miss me?

16

On the Bright Side . . .

My Cinderella cottage is sublimely reassuring—or did I mean reassuringly sublime? But first I have to accustom myself to the composting toilet. In a separate small annex, through a fake-out door of thin cedar slats, sits the loo. Now for all intents and purposes, it could be any pleasant little john. A plastic toilet seat presides over a 2 x 4 ledge of pine. The only difference between it and a regular loo is that you lift up the seat and no porcelain bowl with gleaming pipes welcomes you to do #1 or #2.

All you find is a plastic bucket for the "backdoor" part of your voiding operation, and a tin pitcher for the front. Two cups or so of water in the pitcher means that the pee you add creates a perfect nitrogen composite for feeding the flowers in your garden.

The bucket is equally suited for horticulture: simply sprinkle whatever you've deposited there with grass cuttings or peat moss or dried leaves or, heck, I imagine baked banana peels would work—and you have yourself the start of a good composting pile.

It's far and away preferable to ye olde outhouse.

You don't raise the toilet lid and stare into the maw of earth spattered with decades of your ancestors' shit, as well as more recent shit and still more shit and more shit.

The outhouse stink, as I recall from childhood camping trips, is intolerable. You go in bracing yourself, breathing as shallowly as possible, and emerging to take in a belly full of air like a newborn having its passageway cleared, followed by a gasping cry; the first cry in a lifetime of cries.

My own little commode is sweet by comparison. My friend and landlady and carpenter, Bobbi, excavated from some abandoned house dump another wrap-around mullion window array, with skylights overhead. I add vases filled with pink carnations and purple irises, a vintage rose-colored wooden hatbox for the grass shavings, this set beside the door tucked into a low rise of back garden.

The only tough part is my maiden approach to the toilet. I've been instructed in the drill but somehow the process fills me with dread. And then . . . mission accomplished.

Not so bad. Not bad at all. In fact, it's no more difficult than the use of any regular bathroom. Because it's mine alone and it's private, and it's dainty and pretty, it's preferable to:

— public johns beside the beach
— hell hole gas station bathrooms, such as a few I came across in Baja

California circa 1967. Think brown stains slicked over walls, floor, ceiling and, of course, toilet.

— hole-in-the-floor barroom toilettes from Paris in the summer of 1971.

These were only inconvenient insofar as you wondered how long you could teeter on your haunches.

— kibbutz loos in 1971 when the horn would blow that was either a drill or you were under actual attack via missiles launched from nearby Jordon or Lebanon.
— Yosemite or Sequoia outhouses patronized in the 1950s when your mom handed you seat cover tissues and a pile of t.p. and her distaste was so palpable you might

never be coming out that rickety wooden door.

And thus, with my inaugural of the composting toilet, I settle into a sweet dream of life in the Cinderella cottage.

Another initiation rite: For the first night in the cottage—and all subsequent nights—I have a pressing need to drag Huxley with me into the sleep loft. A heavy-duty lavender ladder is there at our service but, shoot! dogs don't climb ladders unless they're Rin Tin Tin.

I contemplate wrapping him in some kind of sling and performing a fireman's carry up the steps, but I'm just not that clever. Or strong. In fact, on the score of the kind of cleverness and strength that shepherds you through life, I learned my principle shortcomings from Aldous Huxley in his *Perennial Philosophy.*

Yes, I learned everything worth knowing about Everything Important in *P. Philo*, the great handbook for all the mystical musings that have ever been, well, mused. He wrote it in 1941 when western civ was heading for the ultimate cataclysm and yet, when you read it, you realize with Divine Agency we'll somehow get to the other, better side and that "evil is self-stultifying."

That particular WWII evil took a long time to compost.

Huxley shares the three basic human personality profiles as developed by a Dr. William Sheldon. (Yes, I know the "a" before the name suggests he's gone by the wayside, historically, culturally, and he has. Hasn't he?) So . . .

#1) there's the viscerotonic for which, in the dictionary, they should flash a pic of my mom. Big tummy, loves to eat, drink, socialize, especially if she's regaling her audience with her own stories.

Next up is #2) somatotonic, per the warrior class. Hello Hotspur and Agamemnon and Kanye West. You know who you are.

And finally there's poor little #3) cerebrotonic, basically your frail intellectual *cum* mystic. Says Aldous, "—a remarkably high proportion of extreme cerebrotonics fail to make good as normal citizens and average pillars of society. But if many fail, many also become abnormal on the higher scale of average. In universities, monasteries, and research laboratories—whenever sheltered positions are provided for those whose small guts and feeble muscles do not permit them to eat or fight their way through the ordinary rough and tumble—the percentage of outstandingly gifted and accomplished cerebrotonics will almost always be very high. Realizing the importance of this extreme, over-evolved and scarcely viable type of human being, all civilizations have provided in one way or another for its protection."

Ya gotta love Aldous Huxley! Since I first came across the Perennial Philo in the late '90s, I've mashed and mangled any number of copies as I churn through it again and again. Don't know why no one else in my world ever seems to cotton to it the way I have—I keep passing out copies. But that spiel about cerebrotonics being "scarcely viable," it helps explain away the holes in my pre-frontal cortex.

I'm pretty sure I do have holes in my p.f.c.

I'll wager an MRI would show you a brain like a janitor's broom moppings.

Or, more accurate, I'll bet the clinicians would freeze the panel and call out to their colleagues, "Hey, come take a look! This old chick has no left hemisphere to her brain! It's just blank! Black! Blackly blank!"

And consequently, here I am in my Cinderella cottage, my own mini-monastery.

You might ask why I never just drank the Koolaid and sealed myself up in a convent.

The main sticking point is all that obedience they thrust on each poor feeble-boned, small-gutted nun. No, thank you! You can keep your rules and cloistral CC & R's. I'll just crawl up this lavender ladder with my doggy and sleep through the night, periodically waking to stare at the stars through my own private skylight, at times even near-sightedly spotting a shooting star.

All at once I think of a quote from Henry Miller in *Tropic of Cancer*. He's quit all the trappings of conventional horridness—a job with a company—I don't know, was it AT&T?—and a bougie life in Brooklyn—to spring himself over the ocean to Paris. He lines up friends of friends, cousins of friends, cousins of cousins, to feed him. He keeps a calendar of who fronts him for dinner which night.

And for lodging he sleeps on park benches in the Luxembourg gardens. This is what he said about those first weeks, which for most people would pose a horror beyond reckoning:

"I was without money, without resources, without hopes. I was the happiest man alive."

So now was I, for mostly the same reasons, the happiest woman?

Maybe I needed to be bumped down to that last symbol of pure homelessness, pure freedom, the park bench. As long as I had my pup Huxley, I'd survive. But still, the happiest? Let's leave that as the special purview of Henry Miller.

17

A Chiron in Aries June

At the Book Barn I put it out on Facebook that I'm here, so amigos have been showing up. Especially good amigos such as dear Gwyn with her short moussed blond hair and hipster thick black-rim glasses, who riffles over the shelves for cool reading—hey! she discovers a vintage book about Lizzie Borden written by a woman who was a child neighbor of the Ax Girl.

The author states right up front that, by all means, Lizzie did it, those forty whacks and then another forty-one for good measure, but she liked her; everyone did.

And all this time at the bookstore Huxley is with me! He's old, halt, blind, and deaf at this point but still up to a half-hour walk as we loop-de-loop through woods and pretty neighborhoods.

Once we arrive at the store, Hux alternates his time between sleeping under the front lintel, blocking the path of customers, but no one minds; book lovers love dogs—you can take that to the bank.

He receives the attention as his due.

He'll also mosey around shoppers as if alert to their reading tastes. He hobbles outside into the garden, like a gentleman, doing his business in the bushes, but he never wanders out past the hedge into the little back street.

I wonder if he's tracking old memories of our own original bookstore, Sun Porch Books, as I've written before, 2002–2008.

That's a mighty long stretch for a book joint on a touristy street in Oak Bluffs. I coulda carried it longer but, take a whizz at the latter date: spring of 2008.

In June of 2007 I saw sales drop by 66%. The coming recession had me in its undertow. I could even foresee from my own spending habits that books are the first luxury to be jettisoned.

"Let's hit up the library, babe, until we find new jobs." Can't you hear all nicey-nice bookish couples deciding that?

Huxley was there at Sun Porch Books as a puppy. He sprawled on the pink floral sofa at the rear of the shop. On his back, pre-neuter black balls the size of rutabagas were rivetingly exposed.

Little girls would nudge their moms, giggle, point, and ask, "What're *THOSE?!*"

Other times he would romp like the mad alpha pup that he was. His favorite trick was in the winter when he'd jump up and grab a customer's gloves. *"HEY!"* they'd shout, enraged, while I couldn't help laughing even as I recovered the stolen items from his round red mouth.

In the very beginning of his tenure, I noticed him chewing a book from a lower shelf.

Honestly, I don't know why the discipline I imposed worked but it did: I sat down with him on the floor, myself in a lotus position.

"Dude, we can't have you mauling books. You're as much a part of this operation as I am, and these babies here—" I pointed at the nearby stacks, "—will support us. If we don't eat them. You follow?"

He had a way as a puppy of tracking you with his eyes. Sometimes, if someone were within earshot and, just to be pretentious, and to see how long I could hold his black-bulgy-eyed stare, I'd recite the first lines of, oh, let's just say Tintern Abbey—

Five years have past; five summers, with the length
Of five long winters! and again I hear
These waters, rolling from their mountain-springs

He maintained his stare. Didn't even blink.

After that single lecture with me seated on the floor, he gave up nibbling books. So now at our adopted bookstore of used and rare books, in the summer of 2018, he's free to go out on the lawn. It's the size of any modest subdivision backyard. An outdoor kiln marks the territory, but I've been told the neighbors complain when the merest kindling is burnt there. Must've been Boroda's doing, but I don't want to think about him.

Anyway Huxley comes and goes and never strays onto the lane behind a copse of black locust trees. Boston terriers, even blind and dumb and old as the hills Boston t's, create a perimeter. Nothing goes in or out, including them.

But . . . there is something screwy about the Book Barn. On the second day I preside behind the counter, I recall that in my ghost-story collection days, a few people mentioned this joint is haunted and did I know about it?

I'll find out, won't I?

◆ ◆ ◆

It's a mid-June evening, so it's still light out, but I'm eager to close up shop.

Again my friend Gwyn pops onto the scene. She's in the midst of having her first play, a clever George Bernard Shaw-style period piece, debut at the Vineyard Playhouse. She arrives to whisk me off to rehearsal.

Well, you know how it is in retail. No sooner do you gravitate toward the door to lock up, when a last customer bustles in on a mission. It's a tall woman with a blunt cut of burgundy hair, from New York, who's been shopping all afternoon.

And still she persists.

She isn't about to call it quits until she performs a scorched-earth raid on our gardening section.

I haven't yet taken that course on *How to Stop Entitled People in Their Tracks,* so I point her to the stairs.

The staircase itself is discouraging, albeit fun. Narrow, cramped, with a low beam that's probably cracked more skulls in its time than I could ever know of; it contains, halfway up and before it hooks a 90-degree left, a small antique knight's suit of armor which may or may not enclose a mummified soldier from the Hundred Year War.

Good place to store a dead body; the smell eases up after the first century.

As I think about how nice I'm being to this obnoxciosa, I tap my right foot on the lowest step and it feels as if someone has taken a butter knife and spread oleomargarine on the edge. I spin in a pirouette like I never achieved in ballet class. A full two twirls catch me up and send me flying across the eight-foot-wide threshold of the front rooms.

Thwack!

My head strikes the lowest shelf of the W through Z hardback fiction section. *This is bad. This is very bad,* I tell myself before expecting to fall into a long vegetative coma.

If this is my end, it's fitting to be having a Goodnight Gracie in a bookstore.

A couple of things happen at once: Not daring to lift myself from the floor, I wave the bossy woman up the stairs and instruct her where to look.

There's not a single mumble of concern from her, so I hope the phantom of the gardening section chews her into mulch.

Gwyn sinks to her knees, pats my head tentatively; it's hard for her to be demonstrative, but halfway through asking, "Are you all right?" she's elated:

"Holy shit! I just found a book I've been looking for—Evelyn Waugh's *Handful of Dust!*"

Two bulbous lumps form behind my left ear. How does that happen so fast? Gwyn, plus a new customer who just appeared, opine that I should visit the ER, but I say no from long and checkered experience: The doc will tell me to go home, take ibuprofen, be on guard for concussion, and send me away with an invoice for $1,000. Gwyn drives me 'n Hux to my cottage.

I spread out with my dog in my sleep loft and monitor an addled brain without the ER's help, although both Gwyn and Bobbi call every hour for the first couple of hours to sweetly ask, "Who's the president?"

A question hardly worth answering. "Did Adlai Stevenson win?" I ask.

The lumps take many days to subside, and weeks to flatten for good.

◆ ◆ ◆

Two or three days after the bottom step wreaks its curious assault, I'm coming down the stairs when some brute unseen force lifts me at shoulder level, jerks me around to face the other way, then flings me across the same wide lintel that arches between the two front rooms.

This feels even more deliberate.

There could have been something oily spread across the step on the night of the fall, but this time I'm genuinely manhandled to face the other direction and flipped outward, flying like Linda Blair in *The Exorcist*, before my trajectory is stopped, abruptly and with teeth-rattling pain, by a cladding-wrapped metal spoke jutting out from a magazine rack set high on a side table.

I'm stabbed.

I clutch my ribcage and fall to my knees on the floor. My ribs hurt for several weeks. You don't get tossed around by unseen forces to not know you've got poltergeists on your hands or, to put it mildly, a very sick bookstore.

◆ ◆ ◆

The theme for this month of June in the Book Barn marks the last time in a long time that I'm sane. Marty is visiting from Florida, my great comedy ex-husband, on hand to perform an hour of comedy at the Hebrew Center; this will be the hottest ticket in town, and I've convinced my editor in the Calendar section to let me do the preview.

Now when Martoons visits the island he ticks off all his doctors. On Tuesday he sees his dermatologist who subjects him to that full body scan where he pinpoints suspicious moles. There's one below his right shoulder blade that goes under the scalpel, and my darling ex comes to me for daily surgical dressing.

I put up a sign on the door "Back in 10 minutes." This enables us to retreat to the children's section with its wooden bench. Marty spreads out the surgical kit. I carefully, almost reverentially—after all, he is my Baby Daddy—remove the band-aid from yesterday. There's an antiseptic wipe, then a dab of petroleum jelly, then a fresh band-aid.

It's touching that I get to play mommy/wifey after all these years. But there's a snake in the grass in that our mutual admiration isn't, well, mutual.

Check this out: On July 15 I'm scheduled to be honored— yes, *HONORED*, when else have I ever been fucking honored?!— by the Friends of the Vineyard Haven Library as Vineyard Author of the Year.

I learned about this Celebration of Me a few months back and it shocked me silly.

The woman in charge told me, "In the past we've chosen Geraldine Brooks and DavidMcCulloch, Judy Blume, Bill Styron. But this year we thought 'Let's get a real local yokel year-round island writer.'"

"Well, that would be me!" I granted. The hoopla includes reading for thirty to forty minutes—now there's the honor spot!— followed by a tented luncheon on the library's tiled patio, with wine and cakes and little sandwiches.

Call me Queen for a Day!

I could not have felt more gratified had a trio of male dancers in gold spangles picked me up and carted me back and forth across the Rockettes' stage, their long legs scissoring in a cancan.

And so when, some months before, Marty laid out his itinerary for his island visit, which included heading back to Florida on July 12, this a perfect salute to Charlie's birthday on the eleventh and, yes, the jewel in the Nadler crown would be here, I mentioned without ado that he might want to extend his stay a couple of days through Sunday July 15 for my Vineyard Author of The Year event.

Of the fucking year!

But no. He declined. Had to get back for special occasions, prior commitments. And I don't believe he even heard me, the invitation I'd unfurled like a heraldic banner.

I have a high threshold for narcissists in my inner circle.

Probably reminds me of dear old Mom. And Pop, come to think of it.

And Marty is so adorable and funny, it's hard to hold that against him.

In Marty's and my original courtship days, in the winter of 1976; he was thirty, I twenty-eight, he and Garry Marshall had just hired me to write a script for *Laverne & Shirley.*

I lived in Santa Monica in a fun two-level studio apartment. From the rooftop, up a set of inside stairs, you could see the ocean. Marty had a one-bedroom apartment in North Hollywood, very basic, with a long closet, room to hang all his tee-shirts, and he was proud of it.

Years later, after we'd lived in Malibu, and traveled frequently, to Europe, New York, and Martha's Vineyard, Marty said, "If I'd never met you, I'd still be living in my North Hollywood apartment, and I'd have a million dollars in the bank."

He's right, of course.

But on those long-ago North Hollywood nights, we'd meet after work—his work—and he'd have Greek-chorus-sized laments; fights with the studio suits, an ongoing fracas when he briefly transferred over to *Chico and the Man* because old pal Freddie Prinz, whom he'd known from New York *Improv* days, wanted him on the show, but the producer felt threatened.

I mean, Nadler would go on and on and, while I found it all engrossing, I kept waiting for that pause and the question:

"So how was your day?"

Not that I'd had much of one. Morning writing, cycling around the madly wonderful pre-elite Santa Monica in the afternoon, perhaps a sprawl on the beach with a good book; let's see, in those days I was into Steinbeck and Thomas Berger and Louis Ferdinand Celine.

"So how was your day?" Never asked.

He must've known he'd be bored to crap if I told him.

In the event, by the time the Vineyard Author thing rolls around in the summer of 2018, I'm too dizzy with bookstore madness to fully comprehend it.

Funnily enough, on the day itself, I entertain the troops with passages from this, the first chapters of *The Hobo Diaries*. If they'd need any hints that I'm the local-yokel year-round author I'm billed to be, they have only to learn about my failed rentals and composting toilet to be reassured.

18

Summer? Did We Just Have a Summer?

The Vineyard high season has a way of stretching out endlessly with traffic grids and long lines for ice cream and crowded beaches—beaches which in the off season you can wander with your dog without anybody shouting at you to get your bloody beast off the sand. We sport bumper stickers that declare, *Pray for September!* as if we'll need Divine Intervention to bring it on. And then it comes. It slams around quickly, in fact.

But wait. I've jumped ahead of myself.

◆ ◆ ◆

Before June had ended, Boroda is back to acting like a sworn twat. I use "twat" in the English spirit, directed at a male who's proved himself a prime, well, cunt. Brits say that too. All it took was one fell gender swap to remove the whole misogynistic angle.

The son/cop's return to twatty cuntiness comes about when the Barnes Moving dudes bring a few choice pieces back to the bookstore. Well, I emailed Dimitri this was happening, that no good had come of removing every last ceramic tissue holder and matching jar of cotton swabs.

It's just a coupla chairs, lamps, rugs, and a few other fair-thee-wells, and it only takes ten or twelve minutes to drop it all off, but that's all the harm required; it's 5 in the evening and grim Boroda rides home in his cop SUV in time to witness what he doubtless perceives as renewed hostilities.

No words are exchanged, but I take in the bad timing, and know we're headed for fresh trouble. I try above-the-board communication. Starting in mid-June, once a week a trusted book lover fills in for me; pretty Mary with long wavy brown hair, my vet's assistant, and a fan of scary books about witchcraft and ghosts and slithery creatures of the night; and Andrea, young rosy-faced librarian who happily flits from overtime with books at the library to more overtime with books at the Barn, ours being mostly old and asthma-provoking dusty, and rich in treasure.

Ahead of each woman's arrival, I email Boroda and Tami that either Mary or Andrea are filling in for me, and that I hoped to extend courtesy of the loo behind the kitchen.

And bloody hell, it works!

Note to self: Try open and ceaseless communication about all things and you'll face less blowback in life.

Okay, okay, back to the present: The bookstore continues apace without much fuss except I count myself lucky on a day when no blistering email arrives from Belarus.

CLEAN UP THAT MESS IN THE AISLE! [photo snapped at midnight by the surveillant cop son]; *NOT A SINGLE DONATION TO BE ACCEPTED! . . . WHAT'S THIS BOX OF NEGLIGIBLE BOOKS?! . . . RANDOM PILES OF SHIT JUST INSIDE THE DOOR - DEAL WITH IT!*

Which reminds me: I've been thinking some more about Dimitri, of Belarusian stock, that he comes from, arguably, Cossack origins. Now I too have Belarus roots, but they're Jewish, so it was Dimitri's vigilante peeps who pounded on horses down from the hills to burn *our* horse corrals and *our* goat sheds and to pogrom-pillage our villages and rape all the girls from thirteen to ninety.

A new dilemma is developing.

The way we've been handling the 50/50 split is that credit card sales go *ca-ching* in Dimitri's bank, whereas I take my share in cash.

Well guess what?

Now that we've entered the high summer season of July,

there is no cash! It's gone rediculously out of style! Have you seen those signs on New York businesses, *NO CASH ACCEPTED HERE?* Like a twenty-dollar bill could give you chicken pox.

Whole nations are shutting down the supply of bills and clinkity-clink coins. Which means my share of the proceeds has been ebbing away. I've emailed Dimitri about this, suggesting his daughter-in-law Tami write me a check to make up the difference. It stands at just under two thou. She's a bookkeeper at the local bank where his bookstore haul resides. I hear nothing about this matter as the cash drawer dries up, apart from the $100-ish I keep available for customers.

I continue to love the operations of the Barn itself. And I haven't even begun to plumb the depths of where stuff is at! I feel like an undersea explorer of old marine wrecks: Is this shadowy entrenchment where I'll find the lost anthropology tomes? And here, under the soaked kitchen midden, could this be the fiction of African American authors, something for which everyone in Oak Bluffs is clamoring?

Also I've been grappling with the fucked-up *feng shui* of the place. It's been a long time since anyone has taken a personal interest in the premises.

Tami tells me that in the previous couple of summers, she and Boroda reserved themselves for weekend biz, but all this entails is waiting in the front house, where they watch TV all day, for a bell from the bookstore desk to summon them. Can't imagine that a roaring trade developed out of *that.*

Dimitri in Belarus must be chortling over the sums I'm bringing in—not a fortune, mind you, but in the four digits for a July week.

So, *feng shui*-wise, I've restored the front room table with its pileup of Vineyard authors and subjects. I learned at Sun Porch Books that this constituted our bread and butter, or even *pain de chocolat* and *sauce caramel.*

For the secondary orbit at Sun Porch, the book club crowd, I'd organized a table of *Eat, Pray, Love, Five Quarters of the Orange, The Bluest Eye,* like that.

I haven't got that option at the Book Barn because there's no room for piles of the same new book, only an odd delicacy in the fiction section that might capture one's interest such as *The Bean Trees* by Barbara Kingsolver, *The Queen of Spades* by Alexander Pushkin, and *Everyone But Thee and Me* by Ogden Nash.

A huge bunch of the books, of course, are tweedy with dust and incontinent with mold. For all of Dimitri's nasty emails about straightening up, what I could really do to swob out the two grimy floors would be to organize a bonfire out on the lawn which we'd keep going for the weeks of summer by tossing on every last tome that you'd be wise to examine with forensics gloves.

A new demand swooshes down the pike from Belarus. Dimitri, in a micro-managing mode, demands to know exactly what we are selling, listing title, author, price, and any fey particulars such as *1975, 1st ed, author signed*. This isn't new. For decades owners and clerks of the tawdry old bookstore have been handwriting daily sales in one crummy old notebook after another. But here's the new wrinkle: At the end of each day, I'm to snap a pic of the sales log and email said pic to the Cossack barracks.

Well, I know how to use all this tech shit about as well as I can design a rocket booster for Elon Musk. The super lovely Tami comes over for a demonstration. We send a ghastly pic of the two of us—well, Tami looks fine; I'm at an age when a great deal of photoshopping needs to be applied—to Dimitri to prove we're working on it, we got this one.

Later in the day, I tape together four days' worth of sales logs, click a photo and, by George, actually mail it off to the boss man, just to show a willingness to catch him up to speed. His reply:

"What is this mess you sent me? It looks like a third-grader's homework!" Every so often a girl's got to get tough with The Man.

I lay it on the line:

"I'm a professional writer who's been typing since I took my own stab at a Nancy Drew novel at the age of eight. I'm gonna type up the daily sales, and I'll email each one to you at the end of the day."

His grudging response: "If that's what you need to do to fulfill this task, so be it." Typing as pathology. Wonder if that's itemized in the DMZ?

From that day forward, until the end of my term at the bookstore, Dimitri receives typed, legible, neato-keen copies of the daily biz, after years of filling up coffee-soaked, crenelated old notebooks of handwritten notes.

Did I hear a word of thanks, a comment on a major improvement? Uh uh. I believe Boroda's nightly raids on the premises, with photos of stuff like the stacks of old art books on the upstairs floor that have collected fungus and tuberculosis spores since the 1950s, have convinced the old Belarusian that I'm a bum pick as store-runner.

It doesn't help that the cop son refers to me as (I see this in c.c.ed emails: "Nadler" as in [perp] Nadler:

"Nadler's up to something with that coat rack inside the front door."

"Nadler's planning on camping out in the store."

"Maybe Nadler's been drummed from her summer rental?"

Which reminds me. You know the way Boroda banned poor Leigh from the bookstore's perimeter because of a past criminal record? First off, is this kosher for a policeman to pour over a citizen's stats, and then use it to ban the laborer's poor ass?

Second off, I know, I just know it's killing the unsmiling sergeant that he can findnothing on me.

I had a couple of teenage scrapes back in the mid-sixties, but is there any trace of my little boo boos from a half-century ago before anything was digitalized? No, no, and no!

The only bad girl notation Boroda would be able to retrieve of mine was that speeding ticket on Beach Road in front of Lola's, back in '93, when I was late to pick up my pal Bonnie Strock's parents in Edgartown, and they were so kind, so thoughtful, I hated to disappoint them for even a second.

Mrs. Strock always called me "Dear Holly" as if starting a handwritten note to me; and Dr. Strock, a retired dentist, used to give me helpful tips such as, "You're using a too-firm toothbrush, Holly girl; you'll end up scraping away all that pretty white enamel"; to leave them waiting out in front of the Charlotte Inn was distressing for me, and when that old Chevy ahead of me was trundling over the narrow road frankly under the speed limit, well, I had to cross over the solid white line and pass the poor schmuck.

That 1993 traffic ticket was the extent of what old chafing Boroda would ever find on me, so the "Nadler" that repeatedly showed signs of using the upstairs of the bookstore for sex trafficking and pizza on Martha's Vineyard was not about to disclose her hand.

And yet . . . I was becoming more unstable by the day. And then L'Affair Loo raised its indecorous head.

19

L'affair Loo

July 29. It happened to be the eighteenth anniversary of my dad's death after a tumble down the stairs of my uncle Bob's house in Andover, Massachusetts, and a five-day coma at Lawrence Hospital, but normally I flit through that sad day without pausing to grieve until, oh, July 30, when I realize belatedly that the day before was, duh, the twenty-ninth.

Somehow that swept-under-the-carpet sorrow must have stalked me. These things do.

Stalked me and everyone else with dates like that on their timeline tickers.

It's a sunny Sunday and my pal Lizzy has dropped by to discuss joining Mary and Andrea as my once-a-week substitute, should I need a third helper. There's something weird and wonderful about Lizzy. She's sort of a seer and somehow handy to know, even though, when I stop to think about it, I know her not in the slightest.

Just this year she encouraged me to publish a blog on the website, *Patreon*. I came up with *The Ghost Lady's Ghosts: The Private Collection*, about my own personal encounters of the third kind, or would it be the fourth?

It's cool, you put it out there on Facebook or wherever else you blurb your business, and you attract patrons, mostly old buddies with whom you've bundled mutual admiration, and within a month or two you start to earn the kind of money you would for, say, an article in your local paper. Yes! that much!

I've been concocting a story a week, but over the course of this curiously odd summer, I've been blocked from writing. Blocked like Hemingway, only without a *Death in the Afternoon* to turn in once the creative ice starts to thaw.

Also Lizzy, who visits Edinburgh every summer for poetry/ peace events, has hooked me on the idea of wafting over to that wicked magic city next year. Turns out you can sublet cozy apartments from graduate students for a price that would make most tourists coming to the Vineyard cry out, *"WHAT THE FUCK ARE WE DOING HERE!"*

Another treat: before I moved away from my last-year-round-ever-rental-on-Martha's-Vineyard, Lizzy was housesitting this mad b & b with flagrant views of the Aquinnah coastline. She invited me to spend a weekend and, not only did I soak in the clawfoot tub in my room, and sink my face into Lizzy's splendid vegetarian cooking, but I met the inn's two cream-colored roly-poly cats of indeterminate breed, Django and Zazu, who adopted me the moment I arrived.

Django and Zazu are not cats. They're enlightened beings in feline fur.

Django bumped my knees in greeting, then cuddled up on my bed and stayed as if there were truly a time-honored rationale for being with me.

The next morning, as I gazed out from my balcony at the sea over the fields, Zazu spotted me, got inspired, and dashed over. The next thing I knew she was climbing up one of the pylons directly below me, her face intent on mine. Not once losing eye contact, she powered up as if her life depended on it.

I gathered her over the rail, and she continued the cuddles that Django had initiated, only she added the embellishment of sucking the hemline of my sweater.

So Lizzy's hanging out at the Book Barn on that last Sunday of July, the day my dad died, and she's even brought me avocado toast from that excellent vegan takeout joint in the Tisbury Marketplace, and meanwhile when customers concern themselves with finding something, she scoops it out of thin air. The one that impresses me the most is when this preppy old school Edgartown dude, without the cranberry red pants, asks for a pictorial book on the Civil War.

Well, I'm about to dispatch him upstairs to our messy but altogether ensorcelling war section, top of the stairs to the right, where he can root around, might conceivably find nothing—or very little—about the Civil War—but will undoubtedly descend with a tome about the Balkans conflict circa 1914, and a first edition to *Homage to Catalonia* buried under a pile of Spain tour guides.

But none of this is necessary because Lizzy bends down to a box (one of the many dropped outside the front door overnight, even though I nailed up a sign that says *NO DONATIONS* as per that meanie Dimitri). She reaches in and with a flourish pulls out a coffee table book called *The Civil War: A Visual History*, the cover a cunning portrait of, like, twenty gray-shirted Confederates grouped around a tent that could sleep four (well, it's known that soldiers enjoy those nightly pileups).

I gasp, "How did you know that was buried in there?"

And here's the odd part—the Cassandra the Mad Prophetess part—of Lizzy that you learn to expect. "I don't know," she says with a shrug. In any event, we sell the book to the highly pleased customer for $19, and we're tickled all around.

Half an hour later, I pick up the key to the big house in front and signal to Lizzy to hold down the fort while I pee. When I return, the prophetess asks if she can borrow the key.

Now.

This is the end of my eighth week in business, and I have not allowed anyone, other than Mary and Andrea, whom I've preapproved, to use the facilities. I've taken the unsmiling cop Boroda at his word: No one can avail themselves. This applies to customers and visiting amigos alike. I direct them to the gas station on the corner with its convenience store and restroom, also requiring a key. "Just don't tell them you were dispatched from the bookstore. They resent that."

Other friends have squatted, or aimed a stream, in the shrubs surrounding the back perimeter. Even my beloved ex-husband Marty knows the bathroom isn't one of the percs of being divorced from me, and he's hosed the bushes.

But here's Lizzy, who might come on board as a Book Barn guardian, and who's pulled a perfect Civil War tome from a drab box of sci fi titles and garden books.

Calling on the powers of executive privilege, I hand her the key, she uses the loo inside the kitchen, returns, and toddles back up island in her cute pale blue Mini-Cooper.

I don't feel I know her the way I do my closest friends; she dodges intimacy the way I myself will never be involved in a good discussion about golf, but all the same, everything she does is just fine. Or so it seems. For now.

Soon enough it's 5 p.m. I have no set time of closing; often it's earlier; depends on whether I've been hassled from HQ in Belarus; as I've noted far too many times—*wah!wah! wah!*—I'm just too morbidly sensitive to do anything but roll in the clover munching ginger cookies and reading Chekhov stories.

But it's 5 and Huxley and I shuffle out the front door just as Boroda and Tami, both in the official cop SUV, pull up on the graveled drive in that loud way that breaks and pops pebbles under the tires. He plows open his door with his brutish shoulder and asks me bluntly:

"Who was that woman in my house today?"

I'm caught so off-guard, and he's so disagreeable, at first I evade, "What woman?"

With a sneer of savage cop intensity, he faces me with that alpha-male feet-spread stance and says, "I told you no one is ever to be given the key to the kitchen bathroom. No. One. No exceptions."

I try to explain about how she's a friend—

"No one."

Then I insert a few words about how she's next in line for that helper spot.

"No one."

Somehow the information about the mystical Civil War book gets thrown into my defensive soup.

And then I'm brought up short as I ask, "How did you know?"

And, of course, to a cop—or, more appropriately, Stasi agent—my "How did you know?" is the purest admission of guilt.

But guilt of what?

Did I toss a pipe bomb in his front parlor?

Spray-paint militant slogans in black and red paint on his walls?

Right before he turns to stride away, he says, almost as an after-thought, "I have cameras in the house."

I'm stunned. Stunned in that way that nightmare impressions flicker before your eyes at the moment of death, I think of Tami's baking projects—muffins and croissants and chocolate chip chewies—piled under a plastic bubble on the counter, and how my glance always flits over these delectables, but I never take one.

Never never never, not a single exception.

Why not? I certainly thought at the time the minor offense would go undetected.

And still I haven't even once grabbed a morsel. And, again, why not?

Am I so honest? Really?

But I have no time to examine or appreciate my conscience as the greater emotion is one of *VIOLATION.*

"YOU HAVE CAMERAS IN THE HOUSE?!" I shout at his retreating big bruiser of a back.

Tami turns and remonstrates, "It's only a monitor for whoever's at the front door—"

I squeak at him, "Where else are there cameras? Do you have one in the loo?!"

Funnily enough, there've been people in the local news reported to spy on renters in the bathroom. Who needs to see folks on the john?! Well, I guess there's an odd little perv action for everything.

And one more sinister idiosyncrasy occurs to me:

"Do you watch your video cam from afar? From the police station? Do you spy all day? This is my eighth week of working here, that's what? fifty-six days of total cooperation on the loo thing, and at last you've found an exception. Does that mean you've scrutinized your surveillance every day all day to catch a newcomer sitting on your precious potty? And, again, do you have a nanny cam aimed at the toilet?"

He turns away with a Stasi shrug of disgust and humps his butt up the back steps to his house. Tami follows, but revolves to gift me with another shrug; one of wishing things had gone differently.

The following day, a Monday morning, Huxley and I stand at the crossroads near our Cinderella cottage as we wait for a taxi. It's the same company, and that way I can depend on seeing my homies, either Ruthie or Tim or Jake. It doesn't take them long to give you breaks like a reduction in rates, or not minding that you're only asking them to schlep you a couple of miles.

Tim used to charge me $5 extra to transport Huxley, but stopped when he realized "You're one of ours!"

When we arrive at the bookstore, I'm happy to see that both Boroda's and Tami's cars are gone. Maybe I could get back to a standard peace of mind after the hidden cameras debacle, the way we breathe deep to reduce a high blood pressure reading.

It's another sunny day, although I detect a new *jello* heaviness to the air. A sign of the coming August being a bee-atch?!

I unlock the front door, Huxley bounds in and, for a fat old dog, toddles pretty fast to see if anything awaits him in his food bowl behind the counter.

I have a customer almost immediately, my pal Mary Lombardi, short, sweet round face under soft gray-brown waves, looking to acquire some cool old cookbooks for her several rental properties. We riffle happily through the culinary section in the front right aisle—these several aisles actually horse stables for the original nineteenth-century barn.

"Hey, Mary, how about an old *Silver Palette*? It'll make any chef feel right at home."

She agrees, and we add to the pile *The Black Dog Cookbook*.

"Put a post-it on the page for ginger cookies!" I advise. Mary adds an antique *Joy of Cooking*: "Some of those recipes are still useful!" she notes, and I suggest *Fast, Green and Delicious* by our very own Susie Middleton. Wow. A great thirty minutes is had by all and Mary charges the $156 to her Amex. I've been lucky to have friends spend substantial loot on books.

Most people who stop in at the store haven't realized it's still in business. Those summers of Boroda and Tami answering the summons of the bell as they sprawled on the couch and watched daytime television—*DAYTIME* TELEVISION!—it's barbaric!—are over. As the daughter of a Shakespeare professor-manqué, I've been conditioned to turn on the boob tube only after the sun has set and, even then, not for longer than half an hour.

I long ago told beloved ex-hub Marty I'd been raised on a regimen of half-hour TV slots and a two-cookie maximum.

He shook his head. "I'm sorry you were abused."

After Mary leaves—bear hugs on both sides—I do a brief check of the upstairs; oh dear, was that pile of travel books on the floor yesterday? I don't think so. More signs of Boroda's planting of bum clues to frame me?

Downstairs again I pick up the key to run over for a quick wee. Up the wooden outdoor steps, I think about the camera lens that apparently faces me over the doorbell. Yes, I see it now. Key in the lock, I twist it to the right, hear a click, but then the usual unjamming of the door is blocked by a new buttress: an interior bar has been drawn across the lintel.

Fuck a duck, I'm locked out. Presumably for the rest of the summer.

A long humid August stretches before me, and I have no bathroom to use for the hard long day's work of managing the Barn and raking in money for The Man.

I almost raise my middle finger to the camera lens, but that's not how I groove. It's been so long, in fact, since I've flipped the bird to anyone, in the distant past on LA freeways, that I'd probably need, nowadays, to compose it with the other hand:

Pointer finger down, ring finger down, middle finger up.

And yet, from yesterday's revelations, I've learned how the

Stasi operate here on the Vineyard. For the camera, I shake my head and draw a long, martyred breath. No loo, no privacy and, thus far, a growing shortage of salary.

In the direction of the camera lens, I whisper another prayer by Wordsworth that for decades has brought me relief:

> *Thanks to the human heart by which we live*
> *thanks to its tenderness, its joys, its fears*
> *to me the meanest flower that blows*
> *can give thoughts that do not lie too deep for tears*

And here comes a lonely tear creeping down my cheek and nestling in my chin.

20

August on MV, a Torture Like None Other

It's so sticky hot in the early days of August 2018 that it feels as if Mother Nature has wrapped us in a soaking wet towel and tossed us into an industrial washing machine. This is the end. Global warming past the point where we can do anything to save ourselves. But on the slight chance that the end will not occur today, we refrain, most of us, from offing ourselves.

On the walk from the Cinderella cottage to the Book Barn, Huxley and I meander through the Campground so I can check on my dear friend Nancy Merjos. Nancy's in her mid-eighties and, in the days of Sun Porch Books, made the cut as my all-time favorite customer. Thing is, she reminds me of Anne Bancroft in *84 Charing Cross Road*, an all-time favorite movie. Perhaps I've mentioned it?

Bancroft plays a cool cookie of a Manhattan writer. She chain smokes and taps away at a real typewriter—one of those old clackety loud ones—because it's, like, 1949 or even a couple of years earlier.

She orders rare books from Anthony Hopkins, who owns a bibliotique in London. They strike up one of those pen pal relationships that bind people together better than the best sex.

So Nancy, thin, erect, with a pageboy of once-caramel, now-gray-hair, is a Manhattanite from way back who inherited buildings (buildingS, plural!) on the West Side. On her first appearance at my bookstore, we struck up a conversation about the *New Yorker*, a copy of which lay open before me.

Turned out both of us had subscribed to it since our college years.

My college years were interrupted by eviction from school for graffiti on a classroom wall—*FUCK HATE*; I and some fellow SDS-ers were pissed off about a tepid antiwar rally—after that it was travel, marriage, divorce, until I finally settled into enough grownupedness to handle classes.

But whereas Nancy had never let her *New Yorker* subscription run cold, I found the inevitable hiatus, whenever my subscription expired, a good opportunity to stretch my legs and ignore the pileup of back issues for a good two or three months.

That day she stood over the bookstore counter and lectured me, you might even say she hectored me:

"You cannot let it lapse! It's the best reading on a consistent basis you'll ever experience."

Woah! What authority! She was your favorite school principal combined with Madame Defarge, who used to knit while the guillotine lopped off posh French heads.

No disputing this. Or her.

I tore out from the center of my magazine one of those pesky order cards, filled in the blanks, and set it on top of the day's mail.

From that time forward, Nancy visited Sun Porch Books daily and we dished out subjects like, oh, I dunno, hair mousse, Pilates, the comeback of leggings—I'm kidding!—we discussed books! books! books!

For those of us who love books it's hard to imagine any other subject more cerebrally squinching!

During the winters Nancy and her husband toddle off to Puerto Rico where they own a condo on the beach. The mister spends his days at the casino. I'm not sure what they ever had to recommend each other *to* each other. When Nancy luxuriates in her shoulder seasons in New York and the summer in Oak Bluffs, her husband begs off for more and more time in Puerto Rico. Similarly, Nancy finds ways to reduce her exposure to tropical sunshine.

So, back in that sticky early August of 2018, it's time for a quick debrief with Nancy over my curiously peculiar summer. Huxley fiddle-faddles ahead of me on his leash, not apparently fazed by the hot jello air.

I knock at my friend's back door. She and the husband she calls "Conny"—must've been short for Constantine, now there's a fancy name; he'd been a cellist in an orchestra; an unusual bit of background for a retired Puerto Rico-based gambler—so Nancy and Conny are breakfasting at their dining room table in a bare-bones room alongside the kitchen.

Boiled eggs and a rack of cold toast with butter and fig and apricot jam, very English.

Nancy remains standing as I too stand and discuss the Book Barn. My tale grows lurid with the Stasi boys, the tag-teaming they seem to be doing to find me guilty of God-knows-what. Until I speak out loud about this, I haven't been aware to what degree I feel bedeviled by them. A lightness zaps about my head and, as Hux and I saunter out onto the back-door step, I lose my bearings the way I had on the interior curving steps of the Barn, with the ancient armored knight on the landing.

I spin around and faint dead away.

◆ ◆ ◆

Some kind of conscious foresight makes me push through the torrid air to land on Nancy's outdoor sofa with its cushions of a tame floral print of turquoise and brown in weatherproofed plastic. I sense Nancy kneeling down to my level. I blink open my eyes and there she is, looking grievously concerned.

She squints into my own squinting eyes. "Nancy, I think I need a glass of water."

After she brings a tall glass, and I sit up slowly to sip, Nancy pulls a chair close and we talk about, of all things, the Norman conquest of England. I've just read a book about it found in the travel section of the Barn.

"I hadn't been aware that the Normans were descended from Vikings," I confide to my friend. "That's what made them ferocious warriors, but their time in northern France was a kind of master's degree in metaphysics, so after they invaded any part of the world, they did pop-up cathedrals."

Nancy for her part shares a love for the old and venerable Mary Renault novels about Alexander the Great. I could remember, as a kiddo in the 1950s, my mom and her friends going through a Mary Renault phase.

I tell Nancy, "I think I've spotted at least one of her books on our shelves. Is it *ThePersian Boy*?"

The glass of water revives me and I promise to keep in close touch with this woman who continues to fix me with a worried eye.

In the afternoon, I close up shop to honor a doc's appointment with my all-time-fave nurse practitioner on the island. When I summon my taxi service to heigh me into Edgartown, turns out good old Ruthie also loves Carol Forgione.

"She's helped me with so many illnesses! Lyme, the flu, chilblains . . . "

"Chilblains! That's something out of Charles Dickens! Are you telling me people still get chilblains?"

She nodded her head of shorn-cut gray hair. "Darn tootin'."

The healthcare system is in such a tangle these days, I don't know what I'm getting into when Ruthie drops me in front of Island Health Care at the Triangle. I've got Medicare but only Part A, not the B that would co-pay for office visits but which would also require a monthly gouge out of my teeny-tiny Social Security check.

I'm nursing a sense of magical thinking about my own health but, listen, as a vegetarian and a car-free chicky who walks everywhere—or runs for the bus—I'm in okay shape for a seventy-year-old. None of that chronic shit. No diabetes, no high blood pressure, no cholesterol, yada-yadas.

I realize all this could change just because I'm bragging, and the Fates hate when you brag.

I'd hate it too, if I were a Fate.

So why have I come calling to Carol F., whom I knew from my earlier primary care days with the walk-in clinic across from

Cronig's? Well, hello! It's the fucking *gabapentin*! It's running low and, you might recall, I practically bled from my palms trying to keep it going with my psychiatrist who happened to be under some kind of investigative scrutiny.

I absolutely require this brain food, at least for the time being, at least until I achieve the highest scales of enlightenment—yeah! that's really gonna happen—still, a girl can wish.

So now I sit in Carol's office in a small warren of other offices. Doesn't seem to be an actual doctor in the house, which, when you come to think about it, is a dandy thing!

I say, "Carol, my health problems are all from the neck up. I mean they're all mental."

Carol is probably around my age or maybe younger but she looks older, only because she doesn't color her hair or wear makeup or festive little sundresses the way I do.

And why do I do that, considering my devotion to celibacy?

I dunno, why do some ladies paint their walls a fussy pale lilac or acquire a daybed ensemble of white quilting embroidered with red roses?

You guessed it: I do that too!

Carol's golden-brown eyes shine with sympathy. "Are you having a rough summer?"

We both guffaw because we know *ALL* Vineyarders have rough summers. If they weren't having them, they'd be resting in metal vaults over at the morgue.

Or living somewhere easier.

I tell her about the Stasi boys, about the surveillance from the cop son and the blunt emails from the dad in Belarus, the barred door to the bathroom and, most poignantly, the nearly $2,000 in the hole as Dimitri takes in more in credit card slips than I do in cash.

But first things first:

"Well, of course I'll renew your psych meds," she tells me, drawing to her the holygrail of pill-heads—the prescription pad. "But you know what you also need to take care of," she says even as my fevered stare is on the pad and the scratches she's making on top of it . . . I give her eye contact, which is crucial because her gaze is so kindly, "You need to give this man notice that you're closing down the store by, say, Wednesday, if he doesn't wire money to your bank account. Send him the routing numbers and all that good stuff, and you'll have your money, take my word for it. If you don't get it, you walk."

I'll take Carol F.'s word for anything, even as I gratefully accept her several scripts, not only for *gabapentin*—the only one that really matters—but for the other stuff my shrink and I have come up with over the years to keep me from walking and drooling at the same time—Prozac and also Pristiq, which is probably neither here nor there but, without all these meds, I'm also neither here nor there.

Ruthie comes to pick me up in her taxi van and deliver me to my pharmacy, the one over which I used to live in Oak Bluffs before I threw caution to the Wild Witch of the West and gave up my precious gone-with-the-wind-forever-as-you-kick-yourself-on-the-way-out-the-door of your year-round rental.

And you know all those people who told me not to do that?
They were right . . .
They were right . . .
They were right . . .

But maybe with these psych pills I can hang on. After all, I do love my Cinderella cottage, even without running water. I sleep under a skylight that lets me see shooting stars. I've got my beloved pooch, who's such an old doody dud these days, but he lets me heigh him aloft at night to our sleep ledge.

Tony's Market is a hop skip away where fresh salads await and clever little sauces in tandem with clever little packs of rice or pasta that's all nuke-able!

My rent is manageable on this pricey island and life is just a bowl of cherries, also available at Tony's for $5.99 a box.

I even love the haunted bookstore as long as Dimitri gives me a day without the ranting Blue Meanie emails.

It's not so bad. Glad for my new red-hot batch of *gabbies!*

21

More August on MV—Yippee Kai Yai Yay!

I've hung some of my framed posters on the cottage wall: a watercolor print of Mont San Michel, Chagal's groom zooming his bride off to Neverland, and a couple of prized antique mirrors; I adore mirrors, even those my vanity will no longer let me sneak a peek in. My vanity is actually protective of me. I think I look fine until one of those peeks is stolen.

My treasured French farmhouse table rests under the east window.

Here's how I rendered it French and farmhouse-y: Some years ago when my bookstore collapsed, and I moved to my friend's arty airy studio in Chilmark, I grabbed from the VH thrift shop a horrid table with flaps that rise up for extra seating. It was one of those Penney's specials with a cheap shellacking over the cheapest pine, or maybe even a faux pine. I put it outside because that's where I needed it, painted it with primer, then a pale jade-y green, stenciled on some pink and red roses, then sandpapered the hell out of the whole table so that the flowers faded into the now-distressed wood as if Elizabeth Vigee-leBrun herself had prepped it for her teen daughter.

And then I left it outdoors for two years.

So the table and my similarly stenciled and distressed pink—pink!—dresser took up enough space in the mini cottage that I only had room for one chair, a retro-Victorian rocker with a scalloped high back.

This I'd painted a juniper pink.

It had luscious green pillows for ultimate comfort and, consequently, Huxley and I vied for it all the live-long day.

And here's where Cesar Millan and those other hard-nosed dog trainers would tilt a furry human brow at me: If Hux claimed the chair before my breakfast of yogurt and granola, I waited to take dibs only when he slid his plumpoid-butt off to find his latest chew toy.

On that particular morning in early August, when I and Hux reach the Book Barn, I pull my laptop out of my bag and email Dimitri the demand for money, as per the lovely nurse practitioner Carol's instructions.

I hear nothing from Belarus that day. I've given him, as proposed, till Wednesday. This is Monday.

The door to the front house with its promissory bathroom is still locked, as I knew it would be from here on out. I find a sympathetic ear from the ladies in the convenience store-*cum*-gas station across the street. While I have the decency to refrain from gossip about the Stasi son and his pissy father, these gals always fix me with a knowing grin when I ask for the loo key.

One thing that's happening with the weather that seems to have oozed up from the Louisiana bayou is that I can no longer mount the stairs to the second floor of the Barn. I mean, I *can* mount them, but once I step out onto the upstairs floor, a wave of vertigo seizes me. It's so pronounced I think everyone is getting zonked with it, but when I check with whomever is nearby—"Are you feeling dizzy up here? Is it too hot?"—they invariably shake their heads.

"It's hot," they agree, "but it's bearable."

Every fan is whirring, from over by the Anthropology section, to the block-long House and Garden tomes, to History and vintage Travel, to the tiny Metaphysical department (you can see how much ol' Dimitri values that area of inquiry), from the scary bookcase Mary Elizabeth organized, bulging with Stephen King, to the war stacks which, as I've mentioned, I strangely love.

How is it this Dizzy Head Syndrome—a feeling like you've

just been blam-blammed in a Bugs Bunny cartoon; you see double or triple with a fear of falling down—affects only me?

It's a feature of the haunting, right? After all, those two plunges from the bottom steps, to my standing coma at the top, the narrow medieval staircase itself has the special horror flick message for Holly, known in these parts as "Nadler": *GET OUT.*

22

More MV in August—Yippee Kai Yai Yay, Get along Little Do'gie

Because, in this interim when I'm set to go on strike, I don't care anymore, I close up shop at 2:00 p.m., with a doting note for whatever friends or favorites of mine might stop by: *"Huxley needs a walk on the beach. Because he's barred from the Inkwell before 5, I'll sneak him onto that rollicking section under the bus stop where no one cares what you're up to as long as you're fully, or at least partially, clothed. I'll be the former."*

I pick up an egg salad sandwich at the convenience joint. The gals have been ordering a few extras for me, knowing that, as a vegetarian, I'll only cross over that one red-line re eggs.

I don't know why eggs are considered, in vegan circles, unpalatable.

I would never approve of killing a chicken, but it seems to me that in an ideal world, chickens are meant to be part of our lives, pecking around the yard, and scooching into one of those rustic hutches that lean against old cottages.

As beloved pets or, if not pets, esteemed neighbors, they're programmed to share their eggs with us. It's the least they could do in exchange for all that gluten-free feed we lay out for them.

And, of course, an egg salad sandwich for me means I go halfsies with Hux. I bring a blue and white gingham tablecloth I pinched from the upstairs artist's nook. Down on the beach we colonize a central location with our backs to the concrete wall that holds the road over the beach.

Tiny waves the size of omelettes being flipped over in the pan roll in quick succession. There's not a cloud in the sky which delivers a lurid canvas the color of Blue Booby feet.

"Look, Hux!" I point to the sky, "Blue Booby feet!"

He doesn't even grant me the favor of an eye roll.

Don't know why I bother.

To the right of us, a mom with a blunt cut of black hair and a dribble of floral tattoos running down her arms passes out sandwiches to a crew of four, all of them under ten. I've never thought of this before, but will tattoos be heritable; will kids see these arty assaults on their parents' skin and consider repeating the pattern?

Or will a new fad replace body ink? Maybe fleshly embroidery? The patient would need a really strong epidural of the body part being threaded but, jeez, what a pretty sight that would ultimately be.

To our left and down at the edge of the omelette wavelets, a dad with a bald head but a compensatory profusion of red beard, clad in cut-off jeans and a green polo shirt, is showing his kindergarten-aged son how to shoot out flat stones. The kid looks too young to receive this testosterone-infused display—why is it always males who need to snap out rocks this way?—but he gamely takes a shot which falls plunk! between two minibreakers.

This makes me nostalgic for the days in the late eighties when Charlie was itty bitty and we'd visit our seaside East Chop cottage during August, just like any other spoiled rich Hollywood family. It was so long ago and so briefly taking place that in my memory it has a diffuse fictional quality.

But for several summers I was able to lure little Charlie out on sea glass expeditions.

It started with a small mason jar of those funky sea jewels left by the woman who sold us the house.

On Chuck's first excursion, I secretly seeded the sand with mostly green, white, and brown, perfectly rounded specimens. Up until the second grade when we moved here year-round (I'll get into that later if there's a demand for it), my son, with his jumble of golden-brown curls, began to slack off on our sea glass hunts as he carefully aimed those infernal flat stones at the water.

Who taught him that stupid trick? Surely not his comedy writer dad who had the athletic ability of most postwar Jews from the Bronx. Maybe the culprit was one of our more macho pals who dropped by for an evening beer and who must have taken it upon himself to get our dynastic darling started.

And that was it.

End of sea glass interest.

We still plied the shore together, I on my eternal quest for the rounded glass, holding the rare ones, like red and pale aquamarine up to the light as I gasped, "Lookit this one!"

My boy never glanced over as he skid-launched another flatty into the waves.

Even now, as I'm seventy and he's thirty-four, a jaunt on the shore would have us enacting the same parallel play; a specious togetherness but better than nothing.

In reality, he'd be bouncing on ahead with his young and pretty and outdoorsy wife, and I'd be holding a very distant rear position, alone with the sea glass stuffed into a cloth bag, the very picture of a sad and lonely old lady, only I never feel lonely.

I'm a hermit who adores isolation and adores her son, always has, and who regrets our original river's division into tributaries, sea glass vs. flat stones-skimming-waves.

Oh fuck! I've just been whacked with a memory: So back in 2007 when I had, unbeknownst to me, two years left on the bookstore meter, I left my guest cottage with its far view of the harbor to rent the newly remodeled midgets' apartment over the store.

If I had scripted the scene to make the heroine look any more abjectly pitiable, I could have done no better job.

The two most pathetic factors were these:

1. I'd hired, at his suggestion some weeks before, a townie nut job named Marco to appear on the appointed day with a buddy and a van for the heavy lifting. Marco

showed up alone in a small battered station wagon, and between soliloquies about MIT students hiding surveillance cameras in his room, and anecdotes about all the "losers" he lived with in an Oak Bluffs flophouse, he hefted furniture out to his car and brought them, piece by piece, for storage in the basement beneath the bookstore.

2. The second sorry element was my own lugging of piles of stuff crammed into one of those old lady carts with wheels, as I clickety-clacked the mound back and forth from town. I could not have more perfectly impersonated a bag lady if I'd tried, although my friend, Judy Hartford, next-door retailer and therapist, glanced at the pale pink Linen Source quilt resting at the top of the heap, and opined, "A bag lady would never have such lovely gear."

For the most part, in previous weeks, I'd ruthlessly weeded out every last belonging that it was earthly possible to part with.

My queen-sized bed with its filigreed porcelain and brass headboard and footboard went to pianist friends Lisa and Brian, who'd recently moved into a large Victorian cottage in town.

Favorite but no longer needed items like my white enameled, red-toile-etched lobster graphic lobster pot and needlepoint pillows went into boxes to be sent to my sister in California.

A few shipments had been dispatched to the thrift shop in Vineyard Haven and, finally, I took the time-honored method of the community giveaway by heaping big and little pieces—hammock, chairs, stuffed toys won at the Agricultural Fair, a working vacuum, extra mugs, pots and pans—at the side of the road with a FREE sign attached to the nearby stone wall. The items vanished within minutes, and all day long Marco and I replenished the pile.

I'd made a deliberate decision to leave a few articles in the old place, all of which could have easily been chucked into the FREE zone, but I nurtured a strong sense that these things belonged under that particular roof: a working microwave, an antique cabinet for TV storage, several Rainy Day lamps, and lovely chintz drapes covering the windows and recessed niches that originally sat starkly door-less in the bedrooms like the closets in slums.

These scattered pieces weren't relinquished because suddenly I loved my landlady who'd turned abusive in the second out of three years I'd lived next door, but for two reasons, one noble, one ignoble:

The first was that I shuddered to think of the poor *schmuck* who took up residence after me, and I wished to leave a few kindly tokens for him or her. The second had something to do with an unformed agenda to show said screaming landlady what compassion looked like; here I was, cast out, but nonetheless gracious enough to leave a few tokens of beauty behind me.

The worst moment arrived when I tripped over the front door threshold, and broke a vase of sea glass, as mentioned, collected down through our years—Charlie's growing up years—on East Chop Beach.

From the seaside cottage, to our family's last spanking new home outside of town, to my several months in my pal Jib Ellis's yellow house with the mansard roofline, across from Eastville Beach, to my three years in this last apartment overlooking the Oak Bluffs harbor, I'd carted my kilos of sea glass, contained in all sizes and shapes of clear vases, jars, and bottles, from domicile to domicile.

I stared at the scattered gems of time-rounded glass mixed in with shards from the broken vessel, all of it flung across my small front landing.

I stooped to separate the smooth pieces of the past from the sharp slices of the present, and I was confronted with the bum psychology inherent in the process of hefting these shreds of ancient memory from place to place.

Aldous Huxley wrote that to achieve full transformation we

must "*empty the memory*." Duh! Superb advice, but over time all that was material is and has been emptied from my present life, all except for these vessels of sea glass, and it seems that even if I do one day become the actual bag lady that I'm impersonating on this moving day, I'll still be *schlepping* these heavy translucent containers over hill and dale and the sidewalks of town in a battered cart.

On my nineteenth trip to the store, after unloading the latest batch of schizzle into below-ground storage, I collided with Doc Judy at the top of the basement stairs.

"How's it going?" she asked, her kindly face under the brown head of curly hair crinkled with concern. For the record, she wore one of the countless romantic frocks she sold in her store, with empire waist lines and Edwardian mid-thigh hems. I used to joke with her that if I ever fell in love again I'd load up on outfits from her store.

But now I came undone. "It's not that I mind so much leaving this last home," I said. "It's just that it's kicked up feelings about . . . about the dispersal of my family."

I collapsed against her petite shoulder, and she let me weep for the minute or so that I permitted myself to weep.

"I'm sorry," I said, drawing back.

"Don't be sorry! I can't cry myself, so I enjoy vicarious crying!" she told me, looking gratified. Another non-crier! What did this mean for our modern civ?!

And then she shared this incisive bit of wisdom: "The two strongest coping skills in life are a sense of humor, and resilience, and you've got both in spades!"

Wiping my eyes, I said, "I'll have to wait for the next shot of resilience to kick in."

"See? It's starting to build. And the humor never deserts you!"

And so I grabbed my cart and shuffled back for another haul.

By the end of the day, long after dark had descended, skinny, mustachioed Marco and I finished up the last few loads. Around nine o'clock, Marco's and my work was done.

Huxley was safely locked inside the bookstore (well, he

was safe, the last time I'd left him alone he'd hit on an atavistic streak that allowed him to chew a copy of Jhumpa Lahiri's *The Namesake*, but I was hoping he realized that if he wished to be kept in milk biscuits, he would need to lay off the inventory.

I sent Marco on his way with a last pile of stuff in the back of his car. Next I bungie-corded my cat Beebe in his cardboard travel box to the rack on my bike, spun the pedals a couple of times, and the bike wibble-wobbled until we fell into my neighbor's bare wisteria bushes. Beebe screeched inside the box.

As, half an hour later, Marco and I pulled out of the parking lot, one of his roommates spotted us together.

"He's going to start a rumor that we're shacking up," said Marco with one part disapproval of wagging tongues, and three parts glee to be associated with someone poised a rung or two above flophouse social circles.

Oh crap, I thought, that's all I need, to be known as loopy Marco's paramour.

As I look back over a handful of old memories—like a jam jar of sea glass collected in the Cenozoic Age, it's clear I've been even more of a vagabond than I realized.

And what can be done about that? Nuthin'.

Just wait for the next change of address.

23

End of August on MV—Thank God! I've Run out of Cowboy Ballads

On Wednesday morning, I arrive at the haunted bookstore to find a check on the counter from Dimitri's bank in Oak Bluffs for the sum of $1,890.57, the precise amount I'd stated a couple of weeks ago to mark the shortage in our split.

I wouldn't obsess over how he could have asked daughter-in-law Tami to write this from the get-go. And assaultive emails from Dimitri have tapered off. In fact, they've ceased altogether. That seemed to be the result of an email of mine to him at the end of July:

"While you're making various demands of me, I'd like to extend one—just one—in return: May I ask you to address your messages to me with kindness, simple kindness? It's all that matters. And in the spirit of kindness myself, I thank you in advance for making an effort in this direction."

An hour later I received this email from the country squire of Belarus: "I happen to be the kindest person I know. I am complimented all the time for my generosity and big heart. My wife Zoya calls me supremely caring, too caring for my own good. How do you think a man gets to own a hundred square acres of countryside, with a village of former serfs at his disposal, who value him utterly, even worship him? I am Kindness Personified!"

Boy oh boy, did this ever remind me of our current president, Mr. "I'm so smart I can hardly stand it. I've got the biggest brain, the best memory, and Everything Else That's Good so don't fuck with me!"

It feels as if the universe were spring cleaning its malignant narcissists to make room for what?

Not more of them?!

Maybe we can look forward to having some decent chappies and chickies in charge for a while.

The upside of this exchange with Dimitri is that I no longer hear from the mofo. And things are quiet from the big front house as well, which enables August to reel out, as it always does, in a blather of tourists and delay and a desperate need to be anywhere but here on Martha's Vineyard.

Even in my old East Chop-spoiled-rich-bitch iteration, there were no languid days of August, don't know why. A frenetic vibe reamed the air and, at times, I fantasized holing up in an air-conditioned studio apartment in Manhattan, free to write and run out for midnight ice cream at Gristede's, and see no one at all.

And so August loops around the bookstore, with its daily brisk sales and fun chatter.

In the middle of the month, my darling friend Niki—she, as I may have mentioned before, with a build like the Nike goddess in the central hall of the Louvre, with a waist-length tumble of white hair—sets up a ghost walk for me with a couple staying at the Hob Nob Inn in Edgartown.

This couple has long believed the place is haunted by a deceased (duh deceased!) owner. Niki oils the wheels like a good agent, charging them $200 for the excursion.

I escort the deep-pocketed pair and Nik to my favorite haunted hot spots—the Federated Church where my pal, fabled storyteller Susan Klein's departed mama, shortly after her own funeral, sang in the overhead balcony, flashing her typical German *hausfrau* apron and white tennies.

The Charlotte Inn where back in the nineteenth century, when they laid the foundations for the original whaling captain's house, a shit-load of human remains showed up, which always causes disarray if not handled properly, and, of course, it wasn't.

And no matter what on a ghost walk, you can't pass up the

five ancient Mayhew tombstones on posh South Water Street, moved some decades ago away from the Colonial stiffs to make room for a guest bedroom and, needless to say, all hell breaks loose on dark and stormy nights . . .

Then, back at the inn, Niki and I both pitch in with our sense of spirit vibes in thevicinity. I realize this sounds like we're bunko artists, but Niki in particular has an aptitude for deathbed transitions, and she has even choreographed a few of them.

When we finish our spirit jam out on the porch, with amber Edgartown lamps glowing all around us, the couple hands me an extra $100. All along I've told Nik I'll treat her to dinner based on our night's earnings. Now we're up to a $300 tab, so we're thinking Martha's Chowder Company, cool place down near the OB docks, with those tiki torches out front.

"And even if you order lobster, Nik, we'll have money left over, so I'll also treat you to breakfast before I go."

Before I go? Go where?

All along I've known that my exit strategy is—what with my hobo adventures offering me no new island housing—my mama's *casa*, in the California desert, is *mi casa*.

Carumba!

My volatile sister has taken a job in a hospital in the northern reaches of California, so she won't be around to harrow my bones. And, besides, my sis has put in far more hours taking care of our mom. When she belabors this fact, I've finally come down to telling it like it is:

"You like her more."

When I first used this as a lever, she stopped arguing, thought about it, and finally nodded.

I pressed my advantage, if you could call it that:

"Take a look in the old family albums. If you can find a single snapshot of her holding me on her lap, or even wrapping a hand around mine as we stroll through the mission of San Juan Capistrano, then I'll owe you an apology. Only I won't, 'cause it never happened."

As Hank Greeley would have said if he'd taken time to settle all the young men out in the Territory: *Head west, young—old?—*

101

woman.

◆ ◆ ◆

Another office visit with nurse practitioner Carol Forgione: A review of a basic blood panel and all looks well, other than a passing mere shimmer of cholesterol which should not continue to be a factor for a trans-vegan.

Carol, in the third week of August, helps me to plan my getaway. I catch her up on the doings of the Stasi boys, the termination of bathroom privileges, continued signs of nighttime surveillance and, as I've said, silence from Belarus, which I thought would be welcome but translates as an extra vibe of sinister play.

And Carol says with her usual let's-get-down-to-brass-tacks: "When were you thinking of closing the bookstore for the season?"

For a moment I'm lost in a fog of old yearnings: "You know, Carol, initially, I was so psyched about running that fab old place, I had fantasies of keeping it open year-round, like maybe in winter closing off all but the front room, loading it up with great books, and that load could be revolving; in fact, maybe even a table of new book club selections like *The Reckoning* and *Where the Crawdads Sing*; I've got a red faux wood stove that looks darn real and I could have that running at all times. It would be almost like Sun Porch Books again, only in a quieter spot. But . . . given the ill will I constantly grapple with from Belarus and the cop's front house, that sense of being watched at all times, I mean, Carol, could you operate a decent business here if you suspected cameras and microphones were trained on you at all times? What cuts me to the quick is the question of why this law enforcement son of a bookseller should give me such short shrift for no apparent reason. I mean, what have I ever done to him and what kind of a deplorable is he that he can't open his heart to my small humanity, my simple being, a person who's never harmed him or anyone he knows, how could he not, well, give me a break?"

Carol fixes me with her mercifully nonjudgmental gaze. "Holly, Labor Day weekend is coming up. Why don't you close on that Monday?"

I fix her with a stare of absolute wonder. "Carol! That's brilliant!"

◆ ◆ ◆

I email Dimitri that running the Book Barn is ruining my nerves and making me ill, and I'll be closing on September 3. Cash receipts have helped us to stay almost even-Steven on our profit sharing. At the end I invoice him for $262. I fail to receive a new check, but I don't expect to. I even tell him that I don't expect to:

"You've never been quick or even willing at all to reimburse me." I'm stressed enough that I'd pay *him* $262 to get out of Dodge.

On Labor Day Monday I leave my key on the front desk, pack up my few personal items. I've already given that red faux wood stove to Lizzy. Later on I'll recall special tokens I'd accidentally left behind, such as my favorite collection of Mary Oliver poems. Easy enough to replace.

"Come on, Hux," I say as I fasten his leash. "Say goodbye to this blighted place!"

My near-blind Boston terrier stands just outside the front door and sniffs the air.

September 3 is always a day of pure delight on Martha's Vineyard. I have a strong feeling it's never rained on that day. You can see how liberating it feels to leave this particular odd chapter behind me. No pun intended. If I meant to drop a pun it would run:

"—to leave these thirty thousand chapters behind me." And so it goes, as Vonnegut was wont to say.

I've already staked out the month of September for a last idyll on the island. As I walk with my dog to pick up snacks from Tony's, or march farther into town for heart-to-heart small talk with my precious townsfolk, and then night by night to lie under my skylight in search of the faint shooting stars beheld by my opic eyes, I float on imagined plaints of an ancient Greek chorus, and have no idea of the dark furies of mental dislodgment waiting to close in.

24

To Heal a Broken Spirit

I wake up after 11 at night in the guest bedroom of my mom's condo in the foothills of Palm Desert, California. I remember everything about the flight west from Boston during the day, with a stopover in Dallas/Ft. Worth where Huxley, poor ol' scraggly beast, took one of his signature wee's in the airport, and again I handed the janitor all the cash I had in my purse to atone.

It was a lot of traveling and, on the eastern front, I woke at 5 a.m. to effect a last swob-out of my darling cottage, having dashed back to it from the Tivoli Inn. At the end of a very long and dispiriting day of air travel, I'd been pleased to be picked up in Palm Springs by my brother Owen.

As I lie in bed, I try to remember if my mom and bro had urged me to sit down at the dining room table so they could shove a plate of something—anything! a veggie burger from Wendy's—in front of me. But my memory has sprung a leak from just after the time we got home.

And that's when a warning app chirps in my brain. I don't have blackouts.

I know how namby-pamby this sounds.

Everyone has blackouts, right? Not me, babe. But I attended enough AA meetings with my ex-husband, the noble recovering alcoholic Jack, to know that everyone who's spun too many times around the bottle-of-the-day has an occasional blackout.

As I may have already mentioned, I don't drink. If I take a sip of anything alcoholic, an immediate headache spirals where my third eye is supposed to sit. This is probably a Jew thing. For so many millennia our tribe shunned all but the most ritualistic of booze intake—*Manachevitz* anyone?—leaving a bunch of us without the proper enzymes to digest the stuff.

So blackouts? Nah.

My favorite story about AA blackouts was the one told by an old amigo of Jack's from gangster days in South Boston. This dude had been some kind of enforcer for Whitey Bulger, and he'd also had a drinking problem, which he managed by getting shit-faced every Saturday night, breast-stroking home to crash in the dim hours, and blacking out so pervasively that when he awoke in the time zone of early afternoon on Sunday, he could only pray he'd behaved himself the night before. By behaving, he meant killing no one.

His first move, after downing six or more aspirin, was switching on the news.

Had anyone been shot in the metrop?

If a hit had gone down without a known perpetrator, this dude trudged into his kitchen, pulled out the silverware drawer that held his 9 millimeter Glock, and sniffed it. If it hadn't been fired, he was ready for coffee, eggs, and bacon at the corner diner.

So, as I sit up in bed at my mom's, with the desert midnight silence stretching away in every direction, I focus my mind on what I'd done the moment Hux and I arrived home. I don't know. I just don't know.

I also have no gun to smell.

I twitch this way and flitch that way and fall back to sleep none the wiser.

The following morning, both my mom and my brother tell me a disquieting tale. Seems like the minute I arrived home from the cross-country flight, I'd acted strangely.

"Strangely? What do you mean strangely?" I said.

Both describe me walking around as if in a trance. Do I do this? Ever? No.

They say I made no normal effort toward conversation but

from time to time I muttered bleakly something about "Some man on the island is out to hurt me."

Who could that be?

In the morning light of reason, I search my mind for whomever had elicited this paranoid remark. Honestly, I consider myself to be beloved on my little vineyard, or at least beliked. And yet . . . it occurs to me that if you combined the Stasi boys into one Mean Old Male, then I thought maybe that's the Dark Fellow whom my subconscious had offered for post-blackout inspection.

Actually this tells me something. If this summer-long Book Barn abuse were put to my rational mind, I would have to shake my head, "No, they weren't *that* bad."

And yet they must've been. The blackout itself and my imprecations about "Some man on the island out to hurt me" is a sign of genuine distress. The distress of a cerebrotonic who needs the comfort and tender sisterly love of a cloisters, right?

I nod to myself that a woman of greater grit, an Annie Oakley, for instance, could have handled the summer bullies without flipping out, maybe even without closing the Barn on Labor Day.

But instead I'd suffered a psychotic break after a long trip west with my incontinent dog. In fact, my fugue state alarmed my relatives enough that they phoned my sister in Eureka, California, she a longtime worker in psych unit settings.

Should they call 911 and have me hauled off to some looney bin?

As they tell me this, I stand there thinking it over. Now that could be sweet—a looney bin up in the high desert, with natural grottos of hot mineral water and quinoa salads, located in country with high spiritual *pranah*, such as you find around Joshua Tree where people go to meditate and sleep under the stars.

My sister put the kibosh on emergency treatment, at least for the time being, but in the morning she pops round to her staff psychiatrist and lays out the conundrum of my behavior. When she calls to tell me this, I'm surprised to hear it's nothing of consequence. His diagnosis:

"It sounds like temporary insanity from lack of sleep."

Odd how I feel vaguely disappointed. Wouldn't I prefer to

be shipped off to a lovely mountaintop spa—like any of us could afford this!—than to be told I need to catch up on my ZZs?

I console myself by thinking maybe he's wrong.

So that's the start of my exile to California to take care of my mom and save money and heal my own fractured mind, which I imagine resides in a sludge-like stew in a skull sunburned and bleached and crenelated with almost invisible yet beautiful fragile lines.

The sad part of it is that neither of my two new "roommates" can relate to the trouble I might be in. My brother, though basically a sweetie, and someone who would cluck sympathetically if I expressed a small harm, a chill, a sudden dehydration and could I have a bottle of electrolyte water?, is missing an essential gene of empathy.

He voted for Trump, as I've mentioned, and continues to worship him, which puts him in that class of Neanderthals whose ancestors climbed down from different trees than did yours or mine.

He loves this new phase in American culture of being able to hang with your tribe of bigots and squeeze off ethnic slurs which everyone around you greets with a low chuckle of frankly evil delight.

No wonder Trump is doing so well: He gave the ultra-rich new tax breaks *AND* his wild unwashed uneducated base is free to engage in blue meanie speech again. Of course, they've been doing it all along, but they had to duck first and glance both ways to make sure they offended no sweet old ladies like me who never drink and whose greatest passion is to sell books to arguably the dearest people around—readers!

Had our culture really trained these hate tubs to chill out since southern schools were desegregated?

When I was thirteen, I took a bus with my buddy Linda Reeder to visit her Alabama-bred aunt Norma in Oxnard, the farm town in central California. I already knew Linda's mom was an animal. She spoke in grunts and growls and on a couple of occasions took a belt to her daughter, not even stopping to consider that this might prove an unaccustomed sight to Linda's buddy from school.

So Mama and Auntie were in the front seat of Norma's old Buick, Linda and I in the back, when a gaggle of black schoolchildren zagged in front of the car.

Mama barked, "Watch out for them pickininnies!"

Picki—excuse me—ninnies? This word which seemed straight out of the foul mouth of George Wallace got me thinking and, as Mama and Auntie and us girls sat down to a picnic table of southern fried goodies in the park, as a proud Unitarian, I initiated a talk about civil rights. The year was 1961, so civil rights wasn't yet the law of the land.

In good UU fashion I defended our dark-skinned citizens, but the Alabama gals railed against Negroes: they were dirty with dirty houses and dirty yards and dirty kids.

I was flabbergasted.

Later that afternoon, I called my folks in the San Fernando Valley to tell them I bought my own bus ticket to downtown LA.

I got in past midnight, but my folks were there in the dark reception area. "Our Freedom Rider is home!" they cried.

Did confrontations such as these with the Alabama ladies bring all of us together for a number of years? Did these southern bigots mind their manners around us squeamish bookish girls until all of us were convinced we'd found a moral high ground?

Together?

And yet all round their fried-chicken-and-hominy-grits Sunday luncheon tables, enriched by a pastor who'd put in fresh plugs for Jesus, did these homespun folks, up through the last few decades, assured of their domestic circle privacy, long to release the N-word and spin fresh tales of the horrible customs of immigrant invaders?

And did they gasp with relief when this fat stupid man with the orange skin and improbable yellow hair told them, go ahead and be horrible?

So now in the fall of 2018, to be having a nervous breakdown *and* to be caught up in a sociopolitical spider's web of a new battle of the Civil War right under my own roof was, to put it mildly, demoralizing.

25

Further Healing

It's a long soporific stretch from October to the end of December where a diffused blackout on my part is the order of the day. And yet, I'm astoundingly productive.

I redecorate my mom's shabby condo and give a giant *feng shui* spruce to the ground floor. The best job is to shit-can all the hillocks of trash that rival the Palm Desert Municipal Dump.

Vroomp! Everything extraneous and ugly is cleared out.

That leaves us with an ivory-colored couch of my sister's that was getting stained and pokey, but still boasts a crop of elegant over-sized pillows. Adjacent are two love seats from our Hidden Hills days (1960s!) that look as if wild goats have grazed on them whenever their normal buckets of feed are late on arrival.

Three glam but inexpensive slip covers, beige with a background of aquamarine, green, and gold desert-y fronds, ordered from Amazon, do the trick. Plus all three are angled away from the ruined rack—gone!—that housed the TV, and turned to face the ever-loving great view of Coachella Valley with its northern mountain range.

Outside, the long-neglected patio is refreshed with a bright banana-yellow tablecloth over the round table, black and white lattice-accented outdoor pillows for the four plastic armchairs, and a surprisingly lovely black-plastic-clad fence with a scallop of fleur-de-lis design that offers glimpses of actual pink oleander blossoms.

This fence enables my two doggies (my Boston terrier and my sister's beagle) to hang outside while we dine. I'm the only one in the family who cares about involving the dogs, but this black-plastic-clad grating does a dandy job of finessing the lounge area.

Over to the side, in the small bit of patio extending from my sanctuary, my Victorian wicker chair brought from the island, newly painted black, is the one Hux and I had shared in the Cinderella cottage. I clapped it with more of the black and white pillows and set beside it a black wrought-iron sculpted side table to express a love of reading outdoors.

A red-and-white-checked teapot I acquired from the last of my friend Gwyn's estate sales after she sold her sprawling Queen Anne cottage in Oak Bluffs is positioned on this table to hint at daily high teas. So far not a single sluice of tea has hit this delightful ceramic, only dirty rainwater, but there's always hope.

Thing is, I know I performed a massive amount of decorating but, while I can't say it was all accomplished in total blackout, you might call it a several-weeks protracted dim-out.

The other thing is, while I love to redo every damn place I've lived in, it's gotten me in spots of trouble with landlords who thought maybe I'd painted their foyer walls too buttercuppy a gold, or that time a landlady hadn't understood my need to wallpaper, with *trompe l'oiel* wooden slats, her appalling washer and dryer set that gaped out at my living room, but I really am fucking brilliant at decorating; in fact, people have flung at me this compliment:

"You should have taken up decorating as a career!"

"You don't like my writing?!" I bawl.

Anyway, amid this *feng shui* cry for help with my mother's old condo, the larger pilgrimage in this same time schemata is my hunt for—what else?—more *gabapentin.*

I'm gonna take a break right now to swallow another pair of those orange-tab soul savers . . .

I'm shocked at how hard it is to acquire a doctor in the sprawling exurbs of the so-called real world. I thought I'd attach myself to one of my sister's or mother's MDs, but they actively resisted the patronage. You could almost hear their plasticine reception windows slam shut.

My sister's psychiatrist declines to return my calls (probably because I have no Part B in my Medicare), and my mom's super lady-like medico, in the Grace Kelly line of creamy skin and white-gold hair, exacts a concierge fee: $675 up front if I care to book an appointment.

My *gabapentin* is running out.

A couple of calls to Carol F. on the Vineyard reinstates it for a month, but I know it would be piggish of me to keep pushing for refills at a three-thousand-mile distance.

I decide to take it upon myself to slowly titrate the meds down until they vanish clear out of my system. I'd tried that twice on the island, not knowing, on that first attempt, that it's not a drug to blithely cast aside like Vitamin B6 supplements when you're eating a lot of blueberries.

Post-divorce, in the winter of 2011 when I was in bad shape going from sixty to zero gabapentins in a day, I called in the heavy hitter, my ex-husband Jack of AA sponsor sainthood.

He sat on the edge of the bed in the big sprawling boudoir we'd once briefly shared—it was doubtful we'd engaged in any sex in that last few months of our so so strained marriage—and now he urged me to white-knuckle the *gabapentin* withdrawal, full speed ahead, plus to give up the shrink who'd prescribed it all along.

The moment Jack departed, I put in a call to said shrink reinstating the *gabbies.*

There was one other time, in the spring of 2014, when I thought I was whole and holistic and mentally clear enough to ease myself off these pills that had bodysurfed me through some turbulent seas.

This time the titrating scheme worked well.

Every few days I'd drop another pill until finally I was sober and baited for bear.

A month of *gabapentin*-less-ness elapsed until I spent a weekend with an old lover in his antique farmhouse on Chappaquiddick. This followed a brief period, post my third divorce, before I once again adopted celibacy as my bluest chip in the romance department.

Now this guy, an old-school island fisherman/carpenter, had a phobic attitude toward ticks. Well, most of us do. Lyme disease drops us right and left if we're not careful. I knew from past experience that he would ban Huxley, as a hypothetical tick delivery system, from sleeping in the same bed with us so, because I craved a vacation on Chappy more than snuggle time with this schmuck, I offered right up front to sleep in another room rather than banish my dog.

He assured me my old fat furry foo-foo could sleep with us.

Come the day or, more appropriately, the night, and the dude enacted a new regimen: Huxley could stay in the master bedroom, just not up on the bed where little insects could rove in the night across the blankets.

Around two in the morning I awoke to see my doggy's sad face with his buggy black eyes staring up at me from the floor.

I made a "shush" sound and slowly elevated him under the covers with me. In the morning the dude bellowed at me for my treachery.

I don't like being bellowed at.

By the time I'd returned home to my upstairs apartment in Oak Bluffs, I was tumbling down the mine shaft of depression.

Really bad this time.

Guess you can be harried into it.

I lasted a couple of weeks in the Slough of Despond before I realized *gabapentin* could rescue me.

And it did.

I'd stayed home brooding, not eating, not reading, not able to chit chat with my dog until I called to have the meds renewed. I swallowed two tabs, waited, nothing, put Huxley on a leash for a long walk and, just as we ambled up alongside a neighborhood art hangout, the A Gallery, I saw a crowd assembling for a talk featuring photographs of Native villages in western Arizona.

I asked if I could enter with Hux, they said yeah, and by the time the entertainment gave over to wine and cheese and *chuffa chuffa*—as they call it in show biz when extras yak in happy party talk—I told a few acquaintances that I'd just emerged from a smack-down depression and it felt as if I were opening Bambi's fawn eyes to a new world.

Those people with whom I *chuffa-ed* neither rolled their eyes nor made quick getaways nor acted as if I'd confessed to the Isabella Stewart Gardner art heist.

Neither did they press for more details.

They nodded and smiled wanly as if I'd admitted to scarfing up extra brownies at the snacks table, then allowed me to change the subject.

We've come a long way, haven't we? when we can announce the end of a mental breakdown as cocktail party small talk, the way we might mention we'd spent the afternoon swatting tennis balls. *Whop! whop!*

26

Needing More Drugs and Other Vital Matters

So out in the west in the fall of 2018, when I'm not buying slip covers for my mom's love seats, I'm on the *Gabapentin* Trail.

It's November, my sister's visiting, and she steers me to an urgent care in Palm Springs dedicated to substance abuse and rehab.

Well, what the hell, I'm not about to get relief from sports medicine or ob/gyn, so I give this particular clinic a ring and they instruct me to show up as early in the morning as my situation will allow. By "situation" do they think I have a syringe caught in an upper arm muscle?

I report for duty at 7 a.m., the parking lot surrounding the stucco-walled building looking like every other asphalt sprawl in the Valley.

A vacant reception room displays high up on a wall a stenciled quote from St. Francis: *"A single sunbeam is enough to drive away many shadows."*

Everyone, even non-Catholics, even Unitarians, have a favorite saint, and Francis is mine.

I mention this to the attendant, a short plump woman with a blunt cut of blond hair, who opens the communicating door to me. She stares back blankly. What I think of St. Francis and sunbeams is of zip interest to her.

And why should it be?

Over in a side lounge, several young twenty-something male junkies snooze on reclining chairs, covered by tan comforters, all of them conked-out cold. Odd contortions of their legs pretzeling through the covers reveal a hard night's rest.

In contrast to these roguish patients, I'm Marian the Librarian. The orderlies are kind, and so are the nurses and receptionists.

I tell the head social worker that I took my last *gabapentin* yesterday at three in the afternoon and, because it has a long half-life, I might have a few hours before I devolve into severe depression where the head slumps and drooling is likely.

There is no coercion.

At any point I can withdraw but, no, I'm in for the full course-load. They ask for my shoes as collateral. Patients are allowed outside to smoke if they choose, but they're directed to stay in front of the windows where the attendants can observe anyone interested in bolting.

This casts me back into an ancient memory of healing at the hands of a Vineyardchiropractor, Nancy Berger, who worked with crystals which made grinding noises on one's torso, all in the interest of getting me healthy enough for pregnancy.

After a month's worth of treatments which so had failed to boost me from an overall sense of ass-dragging, out of nowhere I said something in passing about smoking.

She gasped, *"HOLLY! YOU SMOKE?!"*

I went home and quit. Anything for baby Charlie, who, while he wasn't even yetconceived, I already loved beyond reason.

So back to the drug rehab:

No shoes, no smokes (of course!), and the morning and afternoon elapse in consultations with nurse practitioners, blood pressure cuffs around my upper arms, thermometers, the works.

Everything but a colonoscopy.

The sweet, sleepy junkies are up and being put through their own paces. I smile at all of them, knowing some auntie love will go a long way.

"What are you in for?" some of them ask as if we shared a stretch in the joint. "I'm flat out of *gabapentin*," I say with a sigh and a roll of the eyes that lets them know a torturous path lay ahead.

One of them, a young handsome Latino with a head of carefully moussed spikes, asks, "Is that injectable?"

I say with a self-theatricalizing sigh, "I hope so!"

Around four in the afternoon, I'm taken into a small office for a private chat on Skype with a nice Asian lady nurse practitioner in New York. She wears a black dress with an old-fashioned white lace collar.

We haggle gently over how big or little of a dose I'll need for equilibrium, and we arrive at a low-ish bargaining chip. She reinstates my Prozac, which I've foregone without even noticing, telling me that it ought to help with the anxiety part.

Fine. The details are faxed to my pharmacy, Rite Aid on Highway 111 in Palm Desert.

My shoes and purse are restored to me. At the communicating doors I turn to salute the remaining junkies. They grin. They're genuinely happy for my successful visit to the slammer.

27

Brother Owen and His Ukrainian Harem

Back at the hacienda, my brother Owen, a sixty-eight-year-old freelance lawyer, at the moment mostly broke, recently divorced, a Trump supporter, though don't let that prejudice you (haha!), has been staying off and on with Trina.

I love my brother.

If you avoid arguments about politics, he's reflexively genial, which, in a family of moody souls, I find endearing in and of itself.

Here's the main thing about Owen's life in the past couple of years: He routinely visits Ukraine, having hooked himself up with a bride placement website. Beautiful young blond booby girls make themselves available for emails and cyber chats, just not actual chats. That way you might find out that other individuals—maybe even males—supply the content. You're charged per email, which explains why these lovelies throw themselves at you, the more (emails) the merrier.

Now some of the marks are gullible enough to pledge themselves to visits to the Mother Country. Owen is that kind of gullible. As horny as he is, and he's no hornier than all other red-blooded males, which is to say, horribly horny, he's coming off a couple-decades-long marriage and, as it happens, has forgotten how to date, has lost the guidebook for how to develop game. Hence the fallacious East Euro marriage brokerage firm, and Owen's pretending that all these gorgeous babe-os, average

118

age twenty-two, with cleavages that could break double- glazed windows, want him for *him* rather than at a set price of a buck-fifty an email.

You see what's happening here? After a lifetime of a couple of steady girlfriends and one long-term wife, he has Irina with highlighted ringlets and a penchant for submissive sex; Elayna with a bright lipsticked red mouth as plush as a pincushion and running a successful PR firm; and Olga, Natasha, and Anna, who seemingly, were it not for a seven-thousand-mile distance from him, would be clawing each other to unzip his pants with their formidably long nails painted blue, lilac, and red.

So during the fall of 2018 he books his fifth trip to Kiev.

You'd think he'd uncover whatever kind of scam this is at the first opportunity. What happens is that the two or three most promising fiancés end up crapping out at the last minute with health emergencies such as an ankle obscenely broken—at least according to the close-up photo—or sloughing up metal spokes from a skiing accident in the Carpathians, or a case of food poisoning attended by green projectile vomiting, so that poor Owen is left with only a chance coffee meet up with the hotel maid from Chechnya who swobs out his room every morning.

He returns home without a bride, without even a remote chance of getting his ashes hauled, and what does he do? He plans a fresh trip within the quarter year. I can only understand this through his, as mentioned, intense horniness combined with a family addiction to gambling.

My son, Charlie, glory be! has none of this gene pool disease attached to him and why not? He knew as an itty-bitty lad and going forward through all his life that *HE'S LOVED! LOVED AND APPRECIATED!*

So in the gambling vein, Owen's got his blood-stained-red eye on the next ball: "Let's see, I've got these two gals in Odessa who've been emailing me, a lady in Kiev who promises to meet me in my hotel lobby without panties under her skirt, and three more hotties in Makeyevka . . . "

Through all these two-week trips he's laid no one, met no one, and certainly wed no one. Occasionally he's treated to an austere lunch with some flunky girl—not one of the gorgeosas with the bushels of gold hair—who speaks no English and therefore requires a translator at the scene, which renders the event additionally dry and dreary. And costly.

Fast forward to a few days before Thanksgiving at Trina's in Palm Desert, a rare opportunity for these family members to get a home-cooked meal from Mama Holly, and we await Owen's return from the latest Ukraine expedition.

He's flown into Los Angeles and picked up his old blue Acura from a pal's garage, after which he drives through the night to the desert, harboring a fever which he tries to ignore through an already delirious personality, swoops in one messy maneuver into two parking spaces on my mom's Merry Vale Way, heads for the family condo where it's 3 in the morning. He pours himself into bed like a melted caramel bar on a greasy counter and, when he wakes up some fifteen hours later, his fever has mounted, though he'll allow no one to hand him a thermometer.

"I'll get over this," he swears in a ragged whisper.

I worry he's dehydrated and stand guard over him while he drinks a tall glass of water. Thing is, he doesn't drink it.

"I'll do it," he mumbles.

"So raise the glass to your mouth!" I insist.

He doesn't. After hectoring him for ten minutes—something he's accustomed to with two older sisters—I leave.

When I next look in the room, the glass on his bedside table is untouched. Turns out, he's got sepsis.

How he caught this dread condition in the fiancé capital of Eastern Europe is a mystery, although the EMTs who come to roll him from Trina's condo to the ambulance to Eisenhower Hospital keep telling each other, "You know he was in Ukraine!" the way during the early 1800s sailors used to run afoul of natives in Tierra del Fuego and hold up a chewed-to-the-elbow arm:

"I got munched by cannibals."

A couple of days later he calls and tells us he's been released. We go to fetch him, but he falls into the car like the big incoherent dummy who got wheeled to the hospital.

It's clear from the look on the face, of the stoolie he paid to push his wheelchair to the pickup curb, that this constitutes a jailbreak.

At home the next morning we urge him to call a home-care aid, a young orderly who takes one look at Owen and whistles up a return trip to the hospital.

From this same orderly we learn that while in lockup O's kidney had failed or tried to fail. They brought him back from the Other Side. My brother doesn't believe in Other Sides, only Heaven with angels and Jesus Christ; it's all part of the Evangelical playbook; yeah, there's a lot that's woo woo about this fellow. (In a different way from how I'm woo woo.)

Finally he receives a valid release, though he'll be saddled with a catheter bag for the foreseeable future. And what caused the sepsis to begin with? Who knows? But most of his time in the Old Country was spent seething with fever in his hotel room. Did he see any cupie doll Ukrainian girls? He can't recall through the daze of his life-threatening illness.

But no biggie. He's already scheduled his next Ukraine gig for April.

28

What's Not to Love about an Ex-Husband?

In late December I book a two-week vacay with my ex-honey-bun Marty in Florida. Why the ex-honey-bun, you might ask? I don't really know; no, really, I don't.

As I've said before, we're family, still part of the original Three Nadleteers and, although we had our sorrows, paid our dues in getting divorced, we've never stopped digging each other (I can hear Marty declare, "Yeah, digging a grave!"). For the Thanksgiving of 2017 we'd embarked on a road trip that involved platonic nights of sleeping together and linking arms through the streets of New York like Bob Dylan and Suse Rotolo on the cover of *Free-Wheelin Dylan*.

I think the plan, in the winter of 2018, for me to fly all that frigging way to Florida has an odd twisted subtext.

I find myself noodling on how I would never have ended up under my mother's roof if I'd stuck with the hassle of still being married. To anyone. The full package of marriage gets you off the hook for all but some weekend visits and maybe a trip to Yosemite where you and the hubby drop some bucks on a suite stocked with fruit-and-nut platters.

We just don't plan things through sufficiently, do we? Of course the spouse is annoying the hell out of you, yet do you stop to think "Yeah but wouldn't it be even worse to be cooking dinners for a ninety-eight-year-old mom who always forgets to compliment or thank you, and who needs *all* the attention, sparing no time to ask how your spine-jarring depression is working out, even though all your life you've longed for some show of caring, and every conversation with the mostly deaf matriarch involves at least two sentences, the first one thrown down the drain, the second shouted? making you think you're angry.

WELL, YOU ARE ANGRY!

And it isn't as if her hearing aids don't help somewhat, but she's never learned how to listen in the first place, except to pick up on a word or two that'll allow her to fiddle-fiddle through her mental files to select, say, anecdote #87 from the first-grade years when she and her five friends who'd named themselves the Diamond Girls would take buses all over Chicago.

But again, when you're married, you're protected from Overtime with the oldster. So do I head for Florida and Martoons to re-pledge our troths?

That would be insane.

We've always joked that it only takes twenty minutes together to remember why we parted.

For this visit, it takes place virtually the moment I arrive, when we lunch together at a Panera in Broward County. We choose different sandwiches, but make a plan to share a cup of broccoli and cheddar-cheese soup. We cart our tray to the table, I lift the lid of the soup, prepared to dip a white plastic soup spoon, when Marty rushes in and sweeps the cup aloft like a waiter who's mistakenly served a poor schlub a glass of Chateau Lafitte when he'd ordered the house Chardoney.

"I get the first bite!" Marty cries, his face twisted with evil passion. And in fact he always did insist on the first bite. After we first dated for a few lovely months in 1976, and he behaved himself, he imposed this perverse custom on me, explaining that it was always the policy, even when he was a little kid; in fact, he'd throw a fit in the lunchroom if someone tried to grab a virgin bite of his gingerbread man.

Fine, I mean I'm used to it. He could have been otherwise 100% dishy, with the kindness of the aforementioned St. Francis, and the face of Robert Redford in the Sundance days, and this vigilance of the first bite wouldn't have been any less goofy.

But I can't stop laughing as he pries the broccoli and cheddar soup away from me at Panera. And, even months hence, any reminder of this First-Bite Rule, and, in fact they now sell this very Panera soup in supermarket freezers, makes me guffaw.

◆ ◆ ◆

In retrospect, that hiatus vacay with Marty serves as the barrier I set up to perhaps see if this precious ex, for all our incompatibilities, could save me from life with Trina. I haven't lived with her since my teens. I circled home from the Pasadena Playhouse for weekend visits, but that was it. I had no memories of her hugging me. I've said before she failed utterly to praise me, ever, and indeed went out of her way to send me an adverse message.

Here's one: It's 1960 in Europe, the five Mascotts are up for another day of Baedeker with Daddy.

In the Louvre, we've swanned past nymph after marble nymph, goddess upon goddess, under ceilings as high as fortresses girded by Corinthian columns. At twelve I have the usual tomboy bod, but small breasts have begun to sprout and, while my long-term hopes are to play first base forever on our neighborhood team in Reseda, California, I find my little boobies annoying. I pray for them—well, does the daughter of atheists pray? and the answer is yes—I *pray* for them to expand no larger than the 32 AA they have boinged up to be.

But there in one of the grand galleries in this most famous of all museums, I'm transfixed by the sight of all the nymph-and-goddess bosoms. They are, as far I could see, no more succulent than mine.

No really.

That's what it looks like to me.

Maybe it's because my own tiny buds loom large in my imagination, but all of these classical chests are also diminutive.

I slouch up to my mother. "Mom! How come all these statues have breasts no bigger than mine?"

She's shocked. Looking back, I can see that her lack of mommy hormones prevents her from interpreting this weird chest comparison for what it was: a twelve-year-old—and don't forget, this is in the days when twelve-year-olds are still children, blessed children, not junior Barbies with cell phones and dating apps, and this child wants only to go on playing baseball, occasionally being tapped for pitcher, I've got a decent fast ball! and who, now in Rome, crushes on a boy named Byron in the American enclave of Vigna Clara, but who desires no more than a distant gaze from him across the school bus.

My mom does several up-and-down once-overs of the marble nymphs in our vicinity and, as if threatened for their feminine dignity which has reigned down through twelve centuries, protests: "Their breasts are far more sizable than yours!"

As if what I carry in my Dodgers tee-shirt is a disgrace to females everywhere. And what gives me, with my infinitesimal ladybug tits, the right to hold the magnifying glass up to mine and then theirs, immortal as they are, and dare to discern any comparison?

Do you grok why this has rubbed me the wrong way down through the ages?

There was no mommy there to see the aching slugger with her dilemma, who could have known me well enough to brush back my bangs and say soothingly, "Don't worry, darling, you've still got many seasons ahead of you without your breasts getting in the way. And while these statues have bosoms that aren't much larger because, you see, for some reason those Classic sculptors had a reluctance to carve big bopping jugs, you needn't worry for a while that the changes in your body will interfere with the last fun chapter of your childhood. So enjoy it!"

Instead what I receive from this woman is an utter lack of her sense of my own wee humanity.

My *humanity*. Where is it?!

Did I have a humanity?!

Do I have one now?!

On the other hand, after my dad died in the summer of 2000, she was able to channel some affection my way. I was fifty-one years of age and I remember thinking, "Well, better late than never. She wants to be my mama? I'll take her!"

When I return from Florida in early January of 2019, I'm visited by demonic possession. That's what it feels like because I'm normally self-contained, if not always kind, at least willing to talk things through. Mild-style mediation *c'est moi*. But suddenly for a week and a half I proffer outbursts, raggedy and mean, that seem to come from Hades itself:

"ALL MY LIFE I'VE BEEN WAITING FOR YOU TO SAY ONE TRUE THING!"

"HERE ARE THE ORANGES YOU ASKED FOR. HUH? HUH? WELL, YOU'LL THANK ME LATER!"

"EITHER YOU'RE NOT HEARING ME AND I HAVE TO SHOUT REPEATED REPEATS OR YOU DO HEAR BUT STARE AT ME SO BLANKLY THAT I CAN'T TELL IF WHATEVER I SAID WENT OVER OR NOT!"

In the end my sister intervenes from Eureka, telling me to stop hollering at Trina. I know I shouldn't be going off on her, but I can't help myself, I've turned into a seventy-one-year-old Linda Blair spewing hatred on behalf of the Devil.

I take serious action, engaging an eleven-year-old therapist, long straight brown hair, tall, no makeup, my darling Michele, through Jewish Family Service in Palm Springs.

In truth I think she's graduated junior high school and, a wise old millennial the same age as my son, she displays that deep-seated calm and even-handedness. About our country's roiling politics, I offer the doomsday scenario that we may have come to the End of Days. Michele says with a serene expression—my God! is she woke?!—"Everything will be well. Or it won't."

29

My Home's in the Highlands, or At Least It's Not Here

When I leave Michele after my weekly visits, all is indeed well, in fact Highway 111 glistens in the last afternoon air. Sometimes a wind swoops over the San Gorgonios at my back, and the shifting light brings renewed attention to details, making it feel as if I've never seen any of this marvelous landscape before; the steel-silver spire of St. Theresa on Ramon Road, those juniper hedges in need of a shave under millionaires' stone walls, a fountain whose spray looks blood-red at sunset where the gusts rile them from the west.

Of equal help, or even more help, or ALL help, is the metaphysical sustenance I receive from the Center for Spiritual Living down the hill, over to the east, then down the hill some more from my mom's condo. They've got 'em all over the country, part of that New Thought jazz from the 1920s, 1930s wherein Christians are saying, no more dogma, no more hell-fire, no more excessive Jesus rap, in fact let's bellow a big FUCK YOU to materialism and false status.

It's only God that matters.

Let's find a way to wake up with Infinite Mind shimmering all around us, and let us try to carry that consciousness throughout the day.

Lest this sound like a cult, heaven forfend!, it isn't any more cult-y than dear Marianne Williamson's valiant attempt to bring

"LOVE" to the Democratic debates. The Center for Spiritual Living, or CSL, yielded Louise Hay with her "You CAN heal your life" to the mild theology behind AA meetings, to The Secret which I personally find to be way too much about the creative visualization of that loaded new BMW rolling into your driveway, but still, it cleaned the Christian clubhouse of all its allergenic Bible blatherings and brought our culture tolerance for all. Or tries to.

I must admit that earlier visits to the Palm Desert CSL made me think the services were far too platitudinous—and they were—unless Rev. Joe Hooper presided; gay, funny, edgy, married to a man, and all that good stuff.

The assistant ministers tend to sound as non-contemplative as, well, hey! as Marianne Williamson sending up her Bronx cheers for LOVE, bless her heart.

All the same, coming into this liberal God-based field in the winter of My NervousBreakdown, living with Trina, who in her elderly narcissism sometimes reminds me of having Donald Trump for a mum, and with memories of my college-professor-before-he-became-a-Hollywood-writer atheist dad, also self-centered, raising a mystic daughter who his wife warned him not to indulge because the Power of Trina's Pussy packed more clout than a little girl's out-stretched arms—because, at that earliest age, when this same daughter-seeker occasionally lofted a theory about a divine Source, and she would get squashed by his abler reasoning abilities—abler when he was thirty-six and she seven—then is it not, decades later, SO REWARDING to embed herself in a Sunday ceremony—plus many weekly classes, book groups, workshops, and so on—where it's shouted to the skies that *GOD IS ALL THERE IS?!*

God. Is. All. There. Is.

Funnily, I can't elaborate on this faith to my eleven-year-old therapist because her mandate is strictly secular. But never mind! Rev. Joe is on the Mystic Button and so are Aldous Huxley and Ramakrishna.

Doc Michelle has more concrete plans for me.

"Holly," she says one day in her bright pert manner, pulling her chair closer in one of the cozy offices of Jewish Family Services. "I think you should plan something fun for yourself. Some kind of a getaway. You need an event to look forward to."

And so a plot is now officially a-foot.

Back on the island, my sort-of-pal Lizzy has kept popping up to proffer a darn good plan.

You may recall she inadvertently got me into that scrape with the loo over the Book Barn.

A bit more of what we memoirists and fiction writers call "character development": Lizzy is 5'7"-ish, with a beautiful cloud of dark curly hair, plain features untouched by makeup, more's the pity (and I say this as someone who is rarely seen without a thick palette of eye shadow, mascara, in fact, the works!), a portly figure, and in times to come I will watch with awe as she chows down the healthiest dishes *chomp! chomp! chomp!* as if she needs to devour a mountain of cabbage and potatoes before making a massive dent in a platter of rice enlivened with caraway seeds and parsley and basil, then a fresh onslaught of three separate fresh salads and man! oh man! could this baby pack on the nutrients, and it's all healthy, and she prepares it all. Lizzy is talented at everything she sets her sights on, almost as if . . .

Was there a bargain struck at the crossroads at midnight? Never mind.

I'm getting ahead of myself.

She is, according to her FB page, a poet, an artist, a peace activist, everything but what she actually does to pull in some *sheckles*, that is to say, a masseuse. Not that there's anything wrong with that, of course, *mais non, certainement pas!*

But if it's truly fine, why not mention it?

She has set up some kind of base for herself in a pretty two-story house surrounded by woods and with a view out over the former Jackie O property to the sea, the Onassis estate now on the market for $65 mil., a price some billionaire could swing with a single check.

I haven't seen Lizzy's own smaller house and piece of wooded land. It's so far in the hinterlands of up island and, too, we've hardly socialized at all, me 'n Lizzy. But I've been fascinated by her annual summer visits to Edinburgh.

What do I know from Edinburgh?

Marty and I in 1979 had breezed through in a car rented in London, and maneuvered throughout the Lake District, with me standing on sylvan boulders to quote Wordsworth, *"Come round me, let me hear thy shouts / Thou happy shepherd boy!"*— and Marty responding with fusillades of barks, real barks—but somehow Edinburgh calls to me.

I know those hills bristling with medieval towers and a New Town built when Jane Austen was writing about all those things which are universally acknowledged; I know this would be a place where I make my stand, or at least one of my stands, or something of a stand before I fall off a precipice with a castle on top.

So let us match up two imponderables. My eleven-year-old therapist Michelle thinking I've recovered enough from the breakdown to search out a fun prospect, and the prospect I keep kicking around with this Lizzy character, that I'd love to hook up with her in Edinburgh. And why?! She does stuff there! She plans and participates in peace activities. She involves herself in art shows and poetry readings.

Supposedly. I dunno.

Even though my heart belongs to Italy, somehow I sign over an unthought-out chit to this Lizzy character whom I barely know and somehow find, if I were to really probe my unconscious, which I'm not prepared to do at the moment, untrustworthy, even sinister, for Lizzy and me to visit the unfathomably charming Scottish capital, and what with my therapist wanting me to recover and live this sweet little life of mine, I send off $975 to Lizzy for my share of the rent for an unbelievably darling four-story house in a stoney mews of New Town for the entirety of the month of June 2019.

I have a little money to burn from the cash saved from living rent-free with my mom. So more cash is laid out for my plane trip, and more for summer lodging for the dear doggies with a woman down the desert road named Kathy who has cared for them in the past.

◆ ◆ ◆

I arrive in Edinburgh a day after Lizzy, and a weird dynamic is set in place that, because she knows the city and has made the arrangements for the darling house, and even met the homeowner, a woman named Roberta, she assumes a controlling interest in the whole operation, and hands out little barbed critiques:

"Holly, could you put this oat drink in the other side of the fridge?"

"Keep your news from America turned way way down."

"Unhook the exterior door on this side."

"Once again I'm telling you, that MSNBC news you play on your computer at night jerks me awake!" (Meanwhile, she's got me so paranoid about sounds from my own computer that I listen with the dial switched way low, leaning in like a WWII resistance fighter keeping up with Radio Free America.)

Fact is, I do nothing right. The worst part is that only her own opinions count in conversation. This means yakking far past the point when her turn has ended. And then some.

I'm willing to let this pass except on those rare occasions when I really truly know the subject, and I know I know and know she won't listen. For instance, she posits that Unitarians are Christians and that ergo—

STOP! I try to explain to her that I have this one. I'd been raised a Unitarian and could point out with great assurance, that any given congregation is Theists 3, Atheists 100, and Jesus freaks 0, but could I get a word in edgewise or lengthwise or cut-me-in-half-wise?

We've planned to visit the Holy Isle for a Buddhist retreat and Lizzy tells me I should drop out. Why?

"You're too irreverent," she tells me. "You're bound to offend people."

And then she repeats a joke of mine—a goddamn joke from my own reams of material—of the time back in the summer of 2010, when I convinced my temp husband Jack, during a superannuated honeymoon in Paris, we needed to offer up thanks at a proper Mass at our parish cathedral, St. Germaine de Pres, for an affordable housing apartment we'd scored back on the Vineyard.

We got the times wrong and, after wandering all around a mostly empty cathedral, then finally padding our way up and behind the narthax, behind the altar, with no one around, I said to Jack:

"Who do you have to fuck to get a Mass around here?"

This supreme jokeroo, perhaps the most outrageous I'd ever offered up, was rebooted by Lizzy to show me how unworthy I was to meditate with a buncha bloomin' Anglo Buddhists.

Can you do that?

Can you dredge up a stupid sally as a serious reason why a person isn't fit to alight on the Holy Isle?

I'm devastated by this rejection. And what makes it all the messier is that, this first week overseas, I find myself looking at the kind of clinical depression that only comes to me when I have no husband or first-degree relative or best buddy to keep me stable so far from home.

I text dear Niki back on the island:

"Please help me survive this. Tell me how to summon up courage from this very low, in fact failing, state."

And here's what my goddess-y pal texts back:

"I'm chuckling way over here because I've always thought your irreverence is the greater part of your holiness."

And then she offers some psychospiritual Dear Abby—or really Dear Julian-of-Norwich—advice for getting along with this pestilential Lizzy, which basically boils down to be kind to her but steer clear of her. And then Niki signs off:

"I wish I could talk directly to Lizzy and point out how God/Spirit absolutely 100% adores humor and trades on it at all times!"

I start to see how Lizzy is likely a narcissist. This with the help of various YouTube clips taped by psychoanalysts who specialize in this area of expertise.

Narcissists come loosely under the heading of psychopaths. They probably AREpsychopaths, just not the kind, fingers crossed, that kill people with wooden spears through the heart when their conspiracy theories about vampires get the better of them.

Principally, they're a subclinical group of psychopaths in that they're similarly incurable.

I often wonder why the universe deals out these sickos like unwanted cards—the 3 of clubs in a game of Craps when a 2 was all you needed to win, not lose the round.

Really, I think about this a lot.

Now that we have this massive malignant narcissist in the White House, I ask myself, "Is he at all human or merely a human-looking prop sent out to boost the drama we're given to spur us to grow?"

Or is he redeemable when all is said and done? Is he performing a service?

I can imagine after a noxious asshole like Trump dies, he's sent to a bardo like a theater green room where defunct players applaud each other's recent star turns:

"You really killed it with the racism, dude; you one-upped ol'Adolph!"

And El Trumpo would shake his head, "I feel awful about that whole gig. Next I'm coming back as a barefoot saint mendicant in India—if they'll let me. I've been told I went beyond my service contract. Just like Osama bin Laden did."

"What do you mean just like Osama bin Laden?!" one of the fawning players might ask.

The Trump ghoul would shrug, "They only needed him to blow up a government building, like a military barracks. Even the attempt on the Pentagon was pushing it too far on Bin Laden's part."

So Edinburgh.

After the Holy Isle rejection, Lizzy and I keep strict separate schedules. At one of the scads of charity shops on Leith Walk I buy a pink straw bonnet that cheers me up enormously, and soon afterward find a pink faux leather handbag to lug all my books, picnic snacks, and other crap around.

Lizzy has friends in the city—really, quite nice friends; she keeps her "Hello! I'm here and I'm cute!" personality on tap for them.

Per all those activities that seem to define her time in that magical place of crumbling but not crumbled castles on every bluff, nothing truly materializes with her own stamp on it. Her one attempt at a peace event lures no people, and she cancels.

I do enjoy my couple of times at a writers' group that meets above a pub and cafe way out east on Princes Street. Of a dozen participants, 80% or more are male, all professionals, and bearing that Scottish stamp of "Let's have a balls-up blast and be mates and not get tizzied about the criticism."

One bloke named Angus, who has a bunch of books to his credit, tells a woman, also named Holly, from Brooklyn, that the story she just read strikes him as "charmless." She seems not to mind. The whole virtue of the group, for me, is a realization that we all write different stuff and this fellah who pens thrillers would take no shine to this person's romances, but who cares? Some people somewhere would enjoy what you churned out.

Just for fun, I read a few pages of this, my HOBO DIARIES, and Angus and others find it "engaging."

See? No matter what, I've got half-dozen fans in Edinburra.

30

My Wild All-Consuming Summer

Is it good to return home, home being Martha's Vineyard, after a long time away? Or confusing as fuck?

I've been AWOL for the nine months of looking after my (now) ninety-nine-year-old mom, so I forget how nut-so it can be to come back on July 4.

In Wood's Hole I board a noon ferry so stuffed with people, we resemble a turkey's gullet at Thanksgiving. When we dock, we flare out in long lines that dribble into a packed town, crowded beaches, and shops that could use museum guards to clock folks in and out.

So onward and upward with more adventures with Lizzy, who I still distrust even though we've learned to get along in an over-cordial sort of way. Now when I look back on that first week in Edinburgh, when she banished me from the Holy Isle retreat, another behavioral trait still stands out as a horror movie reminder to *GET OUT!* and that was the way she'd started to yammer nonstop.

None of us can stand a nonstop yammerer, can we?! I had landed a day after she did, so both of us were undoubtedly spewing jet lag mania. I for one had endured, right out of the gate, or not out of the gate, a canceled flight at Palm Springs that necessitated a two-hour van ride to Ontario airport in the barren desert fringes of East LA. After that we popped off to Phoenix, then a long-assed haul to Heathrow, London, then finally a puddle jump to Edinburgh. Was this twenty-six hours later, as itemized on the itinerary, or three months and five days?

Later when I finally hooked up with Lizzy at Marks & Spenser's outside Edinburgh airport, she asked me how I'd fared in Customs.

Whoops! I scratched my head, retracing my steps in the UK. Honestly, I'd had my passport scrutinized at the security checks, but failed to recall, amid the endless, empty corridors I'd somehow perhaps mistakenly trod, any sort of a Customs experience whatsoever.

What the hey. There could be some fallout a month from now at the tail end of my trip, and I even imagined security agents asking me to recreate my whole misguided route from Phoenix and beyond so they could close up whatever dark matter of the Rabbit Hole in the UK airport had led to me accidentally eluding Customs, but I'd worry about this in the far far distant future.

Thing is, I found Lizzy couldn't stop yammering. I'd watch her eyes, waiting for a micro-moment of eye contact, but there was none. She yammered to the moon and the stars and every rug and beam in the household, but she never fucking looked at me.

What did this mean?

Even after I was banished from the Holy Isle, I kept things light and we actually had some good times, both of us taking pains to avoid each other as much as possible.

And then came our proposed two months in Aquinnah.

She asked me to keep secret the location. So okay. Seems these kinds of John le Carré hush-hush arrangements accompany you everywhere you dwell on MV.

But for the beginning forty-eight hours, I'm restored to dear Oak Bluffs. To celebrate, I book a room at the Tivoli Inn on Upper Circuit. As I may have mentioned, it's a Nadler tradition to spend the first night here; in fact, my beloved ex-husband Marty has the innkeeper, Lisa K., on speed dial.

Only one problem: Lisa overbooked, so she bumps me down the street to the quaint house of sister Lorie, she of Third World Trading. This is fine with me—probably why Lisa tapped me to be the Bumped One. I pass the night in a cozy upstairs room as battalions of partiers throng below on the streets, lighting firecrackers, bellowing at budson porches, and singing both *Break Up with Your Girlfriend, I'm Bored* and *The Battle Hymn of the Republic.*

Couple days later, I find myself at my Undisclosed Location in Aquinnah, and I think only two circumstances could have brought me here: Either I died and zoomed off to Heaven, an undeserved gift, or I've been drugged with one of those Ayahuasca brews, and been laid out in a glass coffin, eyelids propped open with toothpicks, to contemplate Infinity.

Point is, it's quiet.

We're surrounded by trees and foliage so lush, you wonder if green has more shades even than gray. In the distance, I see scrims of ocean and mini peaks of far embankments. And, believe it or not, the only sound is that of birds.

Thank God we've still got some!

Next day, still recovering from the Normandy Invasion of Oak Bluffs, I set out to reckon where on God's green acres I am.

Shuffling off on foot along Moshup's Trail toward the main road, I decide to hook it into the tribal community of Aquinnah until I get distracted by a bus roaring east.

Oh right! I've got an afternoon baby shower to attend.

Okay. Newly equipped with my senior bus pass, I hop on board, eventual destination an afternoon party at the head of the Lagoon in Oak Bluffs but, like any elderly passenger, I lose my footing when the driver smacks the accelerator and fall backward onto a man with a steel thermos in his lap.

We enjoy a hearty laugh about this and, once I'm safely seated across from him, we chat all the way into West Tisbury. He hands me a card of his wife's seaweed art.

She's Corinna Kaufman and she's having a show in Aquinnah.

Yay! There's stuff to do back there!

I grab some snacks at Alley's, an old-time general store, then head over to the WT library to read magazines until the next #6 bus materializes. The library is dark and locked up tight—

Darn! It's Sunday!

Only on the island are things so jacked with excitement on

one end, and sleepy-like-the-dwarf-Sleepy on the other, that you forget the one sacred day of the week.

Later the #6 lets me off at Barnes Road, and I trek north hoping to stumble on that dusty causeway leading to my friends' casa. Hold it! I'm way WAY south of my destination by several miles. Time to strategize this senior moment away: I can either wait for the #7 bus, or do the unthinkable for a woman of my aged dignity: I can hitchhike.

I stick out my thumb. Back in the day on MV, a lot of us used to both hitch and pick up hitchers. Nowadays we've lost the habit, so I try not to feel bummed and rejected by the fleet of cars that whiz past me.

Forgive them, Lord . . .

On the other hand, I feel doubly shunned by those cars that rear away onto the yellow line and speed up.

Finally a lovely young island native named Tanya Thomas picks me up. I can't stop praising her for her kindness. I feel almost as much pride of her as if I'd helped raise her. She takes me all the way to my dusty causeway.

After the party, I bum a ride from Tyler Hurd, originally of Charlie's class of 2002, and his husband Brent, to the ferry terminal in VH.

It's a mere hour-and-ten-minutes wait till the #3 rolled in. Sometime later—like, zounds! hours later!—it's getting dark at the WT town hall, and the driver takes pity on me with my quavery questions about catching the #5, so he kindly transforms his ride, which is supposed to bide-a-wee as the #3, to the #5.

My last stop is a dark bend in the road in Aquinnah. I'm about to undertake another horrifying task: speed-walk three-fourths of a mile in pitch darkness to the mailbox marking my lane, Noman's Watch. There's an amber crescent moon overhead and, wonder of wonders, fireflies spark all around me like they do in Disney movies! Since no one lurks in the area to hear me, and therefore urge me to shut up, I sing an old Buffy St. Marie ballad:

I've seen your towns, they're all the same
The only difference is in a name

And the only home I ever know'ed
Was a suitcase in the open road

Never mind the suitcase. And the open road. I'm home.

31

And So Things Fall Apart to the Edge of the Precipice

The first two weeks are an idyll like those ads for the Sandals vacation hotels, only without couples performing full frontal hugs in ocean water. But to be back on the island in a home so dear, it leads me to think I've found some kind of promised land. If only there weren't a Lizzy in it.

I invite her to come see Charlie and Marty's comedy show at the new lounge over the plush—no, I mean it, *plush*—bowling alley in OB. Charlie requests comp tickets, although later Marty says he paid for them. This works out well for me since I'll be mini-Coopered all the way from Aquinnah, thanks to dear Lizzy.

Toward evening she walks around like a grumpy old non-Jewy Jew, and moans about maybe coming down again with the island nemesis illness, Lyme. I mutter all the right "Poor baby" things as ole Lizzo slumps off to her room, and because she's never learned a thread of graciousness, she neglects to turn in the doorway to bemoan my having to make my way down to the show à la three bus rides.

Nor does she think to say, "You wanna borrow the car?"

The next morning, she vamooses early, and I remember she booked a 6 a.m. ferry to heigh herself over to Vermont where she performs all those extra-voltage high-cost massages. Had she more graciousness—or *any* graciousness—she could have said to

140

me yesterday, "Sheesh, I'm sorry, I forgot all about the ferry res!" rather than having to act like a Lyme victim whose condition has now been exacerbated with a flesh-eating virus tinged with gangrene.

Narcissists lie. Something we've all learned from the Narc in Chief, as we've watched how trippingly-from-the-tongue is the practice.

Am I too rough on the malign roommate?

Well, listen to this. I send her a couple of texts wishing her well. Then when she returns, she stops for me in front of Alley's Store. It's 5:30 in the afternoon, I've spent a few hours writing at the West Tis Library, and now I wait under the porch roof before charging out in the rain to the bus that will deliver me, after a long winding road, to Moshup Trail and the three-fourths of a mile walk to the house I'm still loving to pieces.

So in the car Lizzy, still giving a good impression of poor Beth March in *Little Women*, tells me about her awful five days in Vermont and how her Lyme-or-whatever-malerial-style condition she has, continued, and she cried nonstop. I tap her shoulder and murmur words of sincere sympathy. Which I feel. I sincerely feel. I'm a feeler!

When we get home to Noman's Watch, I turn into my dad in his valiant way of proving helpful. She has a number—a great number—of canvas bags in the back, and I shlep them to the house, and some of them up the stairs, as she directs.

And then, upstairs, I hear shouting below.

Christ! It sounds like an army of wallabies pounding down from the attic to pilfer all her stores of burdock root tea and stevia drops. I charge out to the landing.

"WHAT IS IT?!" I cry.

"THE BOOK! THE BOOK IS RUINED!"

I'm down the stairs in two jiggers, and I find her in the dining room. She holds one of the cookbooks I'd recently snatched from the floor—a pile on the floor!—to shore up a loose window where extra air was needed.

"WHAT?! WHAT?!" I continue to cry.

She flashes the book, a cookbook, hardback, *"WHO DOES*

THIS?!" she wails, waving the tome as if she's found the Hope Diamond on the beach, enclosed in a decayed shroud. *"WHO TREATS BOOKS THIS WAY?"*

When I finally realize I'm being charged with the Crime of the Century, I lose it myself. *"DON'T YOU KNOW HOW HURTFUL THIS IS? YOU KNOW I CAN'T DEAL WITH THIS KIND OF ANGER!"*

For a moment she looks stricken, but then her own desire for fury, for blame, reestablishes itself. She flourishes the frayed book again. *"BUT WHO DOES THIS?!"* she demands, as if she's just met her very first cannibal. *"WHO PUTS BOOKS IN OPEN WINDOWS?!"*

I nod at the last of her bags now sitting on the kitchen floor.

"I'll leave you to deal with your stuff," I say with a sigh. I trudge upstairs, close my door—gently; how I long to slam it, but that isn't my way—not that I know what my way is—and shut myself in for the night.

The next day, still thinking this could all work if we just ignore each other—the way we'd mostly managed to do in Edinburgh—I slog off to the library in West Tis.

Around 5, I come home before her but, an hour later as she bangs stuff in the kitchen, she performs a turtle-galumph up the stairs.

I lean out my open room and call gently, "Lizzy, are you feeling better?" I'm only a few feet from her right ear, but she pretends not to hear me, raises her chin in a triumphant Shun Move, then glissades into her room.

Narcissists often deploy the silent treatment, say the psychologists on YouTube. Hmm. I rack my brain. No one has ever done that to me before although, scanning way back, my mom used to storm around the house calling out all kinds of crazed accusations, *"WHO TOOK MY SCISSORS?!"* before slamming into her own room. Later my dad would knock and ask gently, "Trina, can you come out? We've made a little tea with English sandwiches. Holly has cut the crusts off the bread."

A few minutes later Lizzy opens her door and says in a voice wretched and ragged with self-pity, "That cookbook you destroyed? It was given to me twenty-five years ago by a very dear friend. He died soon after."

Oh good, she's come up with a juicy enough plot-line to support her fury of the night before.

Narcissists lie as if lies are the only state-sponsored currency, say the pundits. I've noticed Lizzy gilding the lily of an already specious story, like the time she plunged off a cliff in Tahoo to the lake some 1,500 feet below. Yeah right, babe, that explains a lot. You had to have been put together again with Frankenstein's leftover body parts.

I fall asleep still thinking I would continue on at the house simply because I find it so pretty, the view so inspiring, and yet . . .

The next morning, I rise with a new resolve, packing all that I own in what I can't help thinking of, as politically un-chic as it is, my "stewardess" travel case, done up in a pink floral canvas, compact, cute.

At the beginning of my stay in early July, Lizzy had presented me with six or seven dresses she had ordered for herself and found wanting, all with tags still attached. I was touched at the time. Unfortunately they were all in her size—XXL—and while that might work for a filmy, swirly sort of gown, they're of thick textiles, clunky in the extreme on my none-too-thin but thin-ish figure.

I leave them hanging in the closet.

I've learned it's okay to dislike someone. Do I feel bad for her, for me disliking her? I think of all those lovely friends of hers in Edinburgh who love her. Good! I shrug. I'm on my way.

Outside on the steep Noman's Watch, rain pours down and I don't care. I've got no raincoat or umbrella—I left those in Scotland for the sake of achieving ballast—but the soaking is pure baptism, not that I've ever been actually baptized.

SLIP OUT THE BACK, JACK!

On Moshup Trail, a wind nearly blows away my straw-brimmed hat. I stop and tie the ribbon tighter-than-tight.

MAKE A NEW PLAN, STAN!

Later, standing at the rail guard on State Road in Aquinnah

as I wait for the bus, the vista opens up to black points of cloud bearing down in tumbrils of more rain and now thunder. And what's that sonic boom above the thunder? Yowzers! A train, a great freaking freight train, unseen but all the same chugging in the sky.

Ezekiel was exposed to less of a sound and light show.

I'm the only human in the landscape. I don't care and I'm not in the least bit scared and you know why?

NO NEED TO BE COY, ROY!

Liberation is here! Liberation is a privilege I would die for. Gladly! Ecstatically.

And then my amigo Everett calls from the hospital. He's gone in, as usual, for the extravagantly cheap breakfast in the cafeteria, and over the intercom, everyone has been ordered to the basement. Why?

"Tornado watch!" he whispers.

I stare up at the black arrows of cloud and tumults of wind and barrels of rain and the cacophony of the approaching train, not those cool Euro locomotives that glide—*swish!!*—over the rails, but the old-school kind that ratchet up a whole mountain of noise over rusty tracks.

"This tornado is gonna level Aquinnah!" I shout into the phone before thwacking it closed. Lines from Kabir, long ago memorized and probably now, so much later, mangled, create a theater-sized marquee in my brain—

Love's hurricane has come
The whirlwind of knowledge has arrived
Torrent of Divine Love drench me, body and soul
[Something something] may that sun of Glory come out
And dissolve the terrible darkness of our time

HOP ON THE BUS, GUS!

I don't know where I'm going next. I can probably stay with friends for a day or two but, man, that'll be a hassle in the middle of August on MV, yet I'm free to make choices and my NO. 1 CHOICE this moment is to stay out of the clutches of any and all flagrant meanies.

I'm homeless and I'm thrilled about it—strangely thrilled— at least for the time being, and the time being is the only hand on the clock that matters.

JUST DROP OFF THE KEY, LEE, AND SET YOURSELF FREE!

32

A Miracle Aswirl around My Mother

Quick story! Actually, two quick stories. Will you permit me to interject them right before the epilogue?

Thank you.

Post-escape-from-Aquinnah, I spent four weeks back in Oak Bluffs, funnily enough at the unplumbed Cinderella cottage, now stripped of most of my pretty stuff, and yet still so charming, with views all around of cypresses and oaks bent by afternoon breezes, and Observatory sight-lines, through four skylights, of midnight stars. It also provided the mattress, shall we say, in the sleep loft, for languid scenes with my new lover.

Lover?!

You can read all about it in the promised epilogue.

In mid-August I flew back to the west coast to deal with poor ailing Huxley, still blind, of course, still deaf and halt and now barely able to walk, panting with pain, and hardly aware of me. On the other wonderful hand, a final photograph of us, taken on my outdoor chaise, shows me hugging him to my chest, and we're both laughing, at least I'm laughing and Hux, with that wide wolf's grin sported by flat-faced dogs, yes, it looks as if he's cracking up too at a mutually comprendo-ed joke, maybe about that time we both caught a mini spritz of skunk spray outside the Union Chapel and then, home in my tiny apartment above the bookstore, we hopped together into the shower for sudsing with

Pantene shampoo and dish detergent.

Two days after posing for this shot of us laughing, I had to put him down.

At the vet's office, I held him in my arms while the doc injected him with a tranquilizer. After a few minutes, my doggy's tense body softened, softened. I lifted his precious thirty-three-pound body, wrapped in a scratchy tan blanket, onto the pull-down table.

The doc tapped the veins in his back legs, but there was nothing there to draw on for a shot. The vet, a kindly short, silver-haired dude with wire-rimmed glasses, picked him up and carried him into a back room to finish him off.

How do they finish them off?

Do they press a pillow to my baby's flat funny face?

When he brought Huxley back to me, he held the still-blanketed form, now so still, so obviously dead, and placed him back on the table. I draped my nappy-haired head over my departed pet, wept, and hugged, and hugged and wept.

◆ ◆ ◆

It's weeks later. I haven't stopped crying. Well, I've stopped a bit.

I don't cry when I'm dialing up cash from the ATM machine or standing in line at the Oak Bluffs Post Office—

Yes, I'm back on the island, for good this time, however much time "good" entails.

What I mean to say is that the curse of the whole "old ladies never cry" gambit that's woven itself throughout this memoir, has been crushed and nullified by the death of my dear old pet. In fact, as I write this, sitting on the upstairs balcony of my room at the Tivoli Inn, I've had to jump up just to move around as an impossible means of staying ahead of the pain, as I grab my fifty-seventh tissue, let out a Macbeth witch howl, then throw myself over the unmade bed, before heading back to sit before my laptop where I write some more, sniffing and snuffling, and yet carrying on like a pro.

So we do still cry, is all I have to say.

All it takes is something sad and bitter and personal and overbearingly final. And then, as you cry, you're aware that, *mirabile dictu*, you're still sentient.

Sentient as all get out.

Sentient to the point that these days or months or years to come have lessons and uplifts and even full-out theophanies to which you'll bear witness.

Excuse me. I'm getting tear spatter all over my keyboard.

Now my mom could drop now, and I do believe I'd be only marginally saddened. Death itself would knock at my door and I'd answer with a sigh and a deep regret, if only because I've known her so very damn long, which in and of itself conveys freight-sized suffering.

But something happened.

Before I left the desert I sat in on a sacred circle at the Center for Spiritual Living.

This one is led by a tall, thin, striking woman, long wavy brown hair, high platform sandals, named Dale Ollansky, a practitioner, which means she's a kind of minister-in-training.

Dale mentioned she'd recently devoured a book that helped her manage her constant anxiety: *Wounds into Wisdom: Intergenerational Trauma in Jewish Families*. The minute I heard about this title and the help Dale received, I slid into the empty chair by her side and got all the details. Amazon delivered toot sweet, as it does these days, and pretty soon I'd read up about how centuries of Jewish suffering play out like a warrior stomping through one's blood-stream—epigenetically, that is to say—and it behooves us to recognize it.

Only a few days before, Trina had shared a story of her childhood. At first I dismissed it because I'd always resented the way she alarmed me with her own injustices while flubbing off mine with shrugs and comments such as, "I'm sure she didn't mean to hurt your feelings."

She first offered this up in the third grade when I'd expressed sorrow over action taken by Margie Whitsell, prettiest girl in our class and my then best-friend, when she tipped her hand to her sudden preference for Linda Connolly, second smartest girl in the class, after me as the first. I know it's hard to believe, but in those days, in the smarts department, I really crushed it.

Even as I told my mom the dread tale, the two girls, together with Margie's dad in his cool high-up pickup truck, now cruised to Disneyland.

Didn't mean to hurt my feelings?

But this was Trina's story with which she regaled me before I left the desert:

In the 1920s when she was six years old, and her name was Eudice, she had a little girlfriend down the block, a pure-blood Teutonic diminutive *fraulein* whose dad was a member of the Nazi Bund in Chicago.

This Nazi pops attended daily meetings, and the one rule affecting the little German playmate of Eudice's was that she was forbidden any and all access to Jews, of which there were plenty in that particular 'hood. In fact, as far as Bund membership was concerned, the North Side of Chicago was, to put it mildly, a poor fit.

Well, horror of horrors or, appropriately, *der horrors* or *der schreckens*, one afternoon when Eudice and her little friend played dolls in the girl's bedroom, Nazi daddy arrived home early. Cue the slam of the front door.

The German mom, terrorized for any number of reasons, swept into her daughter's bedroom and grabbed the little Jewish girl Eudice by the scruff of her neck, and frog-marched her down a narrow hallway to the back of the apartment. She kept her hand on the choke hold, even winching it tighter, as she breathed unalloyed hatred in the little girl's ear:

"*Juden*! *Juden* beast child!" Or something like that.

I'm getting a little wiggy here.

She banged open the back door, and continued the perp walk down the rickety outdoor stairs, still squeezing the fragile tiny neck.

Eudice, fearing she was about to be pushed to the yard far below, screamed the whole way.

"Halt die klappe! Dreckig! Juden schmutzig!"

More push-pull across the ragged back yard, then the rear gate was wrenched open, and the little girl got shoved into the alley. The gate shut with a Teutonic metallic bang behind her.

When she first clobbered me with this story, my reaction was to recuse myself from all sympathy. After all, I trusted that were this my own sad tale, my mom would blink her eyes, look heavenward, and sigh, "I'm sure she hadn't meant to hurt you—"

But only a day or two later I read *Wounds into Wisdom,* and my own brittle heart opened to my poor damaged mother, and I could read all her later narcissistic biography from this incident forward. It explained the pulling away from a faith that could engender this much abuse and for what?

From what?

No wonder when she married my dad, he, though a bar mitzvah boy, of the non-Jewy surname Mascott, and she herself having changed her first name to the interesting and non-Jewy Trina, she was able to turn to him, perhaps in bed after a wonderful *schtup*—he loved her size double D breasts—and chirp: "Let's not be Jewish anymore!"

So later that day in Palm Desert, California, I sat down beside my mother on a love seat in the living room with its expansive view of Northern mountains, and I told her, close enough to her right ear that I needn't shout and repeat every word:

"Mom, that story about the German friend and her abusive mother—"

She frowned. Yeah, this was a typical ruse if the info upset her vanity. I would need to refresh her memory.

But once I had, I said, "I've lifted it from your psyche. I've got it now. You don't need to carry it around any longer." On her look of grave interest, I continued, "I'm relieving you of the memory. And as for me, I won't take it into my own depths the way a Hindu master might do because, well, I'm hardly a Hindu master. I now let it out into the ground where Nature will take it to Her breast and biodegrade it. So, do you see? That nasty episode is over."

I had no preconceived thoughts of where this announcement would take us.

So my surprise was profound when my mother's face lit up with radiant pleasure.

I'd never seen her look this way, certainly not when confronted with a particular treat, a new car, a pair of opal earrings—the clip-on kind. No, Trina's response to stuff tended to express her initial dismay and reflexive pissiness—"I would have preferred a Mercedes. Opals aren't for me."

But no, she was over-the-moon-and-the-Malibu-sunset gratified. Some of her sparkling gaze included me, the overlooked daughter, but she was simply boundlessly happy, and a cheerful, satisfied mood attended our last few days together until I flew back to Boston, then on to Martha's Vineyard.

And here's where I'm still fucked up and worthy of anyone's contempt, especially the contempt from all those daughters who, despite family dysfunction, have managed to splash through the rough seas of life feeling, unfailingly, loved:

After I dispatched this ninety-nine-year-old intergenerational trauma with the Bund mother, I considered this about my own mother:

We're hunky dory. Hunky dory for the duration.

Epilogue

I knew this year of living homelessly would teach me some neat tricks about life, some new coping skills, some key insights in how to be stronger. Let's face it, from Aldous Huxley in his breakdown of my own particular psych profile as a cerebrotonic, letting me know that as a functioning human I'm "scarcely viable," to tellers at the bank phoning from time to time to report an overdraft, to my steep fall as a Hollywood wife with homes on both coasts—on the actual fucking coasts, to whit, addresses on *Pacific* Coast Highway and *Atlantic* Avenue—to hunkering down in a cottage with no running water; with all this attendant loss of money and places to live on top of the jumpy personality of Little Miss Muffet, wouldn't you think I could use some toughening up?

Sure I could.

Well, someone as tossed away as a discarded kleenex too damp with snot to keep on snuffling in it, either I find some sweet, too-sensitive-to-live way of offing myself, like floating out to sea with maybe a few zolpidem in my gullet or . . . I grow.

Finally.

I grow.

Maturity at long last. Like the college grad on stage with the diploma in one hand and the tassel slung over to the other side, ready to embark on the path of life, this path called Privilege, Good Fortune, and God Speed. Only fifty+ years later than normally scheduled.

So did I grow?

A year and a half on the Vagabond Trail, after a life of one long Vagabond Trail, might have kicked some sense and strength into my princess-y backside. And did it?

I don't know.

Maybe not.

Maybe I learned nothing.

Time to check the ocean tides and find a stash of zolpidem?

But wait.

I am, hand to heart, stronger, bolder. You know all those recent walks down dark Moshup Trail with only clouds of fireflies to guide me home? There was a time when I would have fled this situation; if I lived so far up the long mysterious island, then no way would I leave my abode past sunset.

So be it.

Just think of me as fussy little great-aunt Eleanor whom one of the nieces or nephews needs to pick up, should her presence be desired at a family event.

Which it wouldn't be.

And if I were not empowered only by walks down dark roads, what about those terrible upsets of life that come around with striking regularity? And why such a plentiful supply of these upsets?! Why can't we have even a few peaceful days, 100% peaceful?

Even one peaceful day?

Well, maybe I'd've had them if I'd married a claims adjustor and I'd worked in ladies sportswear at Macy's, and now we'd retired and lived full-time in our white-and-beige home in the Boston exurbs, and all I had to do was make hubby turkey sandwiches for lunch, and he'd take me out for pizza twice a week.

Holy hell, I'm getting nauseous describing this!

Not just saying this. If I read it a second time, I'll hafta heave.

I'm a gypsy pure and simple, these days more than ever, and if every few weeks I gotta take up my knapsack and wander down the road, then hitchhike, then wander some more to a lakeside marina with cheap, only ever-so-moldy cabins, well then I'd pay for it with my usual neurotic fallback into depression, because I can handle change only after a period of croaking *"HELP ME"* to no one I've ever known who really felt like picking me up from the pavement, after which I'd be fine and gloating over this fun new situation.

And when it gets tired? I'll take to the road again. And you know what I've learned to do? Whomever may have upset me, I'll call out over my shoulder, "I forgive you!"

And this new stronger part I like, that part where inside my silly seventy-one-year-old frail rickety hide, Popeye eats his spinach and *boing-a-boing*, his biceps expand in a way that gets Olive's eyes telescoping out.

Like, this morning I received a call from the editor-in-chief of my newspaper who wanted me to know, "Hey, Holly, that turtle story? Yesterday one of the park rangers came in and complained about all the wildlife data you left out."

I said I'd try harder and then he softened and told me how much they'd enjoyed the charm of the story. Well, no shit! It made the cover of the Community section, along with a pretty green-shaded photo of my turtle-darling Dora!

A year ago I would have brooded about this for a few days. I would have entertained some fantasies about this park ranger pill, and these fantasies would have left her, well, not dead in a ditch, but stranded and in need of mercurochrome for scratches on her arms, and when she asked me to write about her again, I'd say some polite equivalent of "No fucking way!"

I might even have prepared a plan for quitting my twelve years-long relationship with one of the last self-sustaining newspapers in America to take my snit fit on the road.

But, no, I bounced back, called Gwyn, sneered at the drippy park ranger before I told her about how the night before I lost my virginity on a private beach on the South Shore.

L-l-l-lost my virginity?

Well, in a manner of speaking, after you've desisted from sex for so many years, what happens when you find yourself on a deserted cove at night, a half-moon sucking up peach-hued light from the demobilized sun, stretched out on a blanket with the one man on the island you'd long thought could be your soulmate, and the desire you've suppressed for so long for the sake of transmuting it into love of the Lord—not *that* Lord, more like Lord Krishna—but discovered instead that true desire experienced in the arms of a manly lover does nothing to cancel out the Lord, but is instead Lord-enhancing, well then—

HOLD YOUR BLOODY HORSES!

Is this fucking book a romance or even a bodice ripper?

Does the attention of a dude stamp *Happy Ending* on my tale?

No.

No.

No.

Although my bodice has been substantially, or at least metaphorically ripped in the last few soul-stirring days.

Is this new romantic fling a sign of the strength of character described above? Maybe. How the hell should I know?

Am I an expert on mental enrichment and bodices and tongues and . . .

Never mind. I'm still a vagabond always ready for the open road. Or maybe the open sea. My lover dwells on a houseboat in a saltwater inlet surrounded by only a handful of far-flung houses, each with its own tiffany of night lights and that moon growing bigger by the day, still sucking at the pale apricot light left by the sun and . . . sorry.

That word "sucking" side-tracked me.

No, this unexpected affair will not supply the answer, mostly because I'm already finding that a regression to romance awakens the lululemon of a teenager in me, replete with all the insecurities of thoughts such as, "He hasn't texted me in a whole day and when he did it was a bulletin about pouring concrete and fitting rebar!" and other stupid shit.

He and I are on similar spiritual paths, East-leaning and all that, and this reveals to us that we're a good match as long-term comrades. Long-term with perhaps a touch of romantic drizzle.

St. Francis and Santa Clara. Heloise and Abelard.

Dante and Beatrice.

Derek Jacobi and Sincead O'Connor in *Much Ado about Nothing* at the NationalTheater, summer of 1983, a production so polished and perfectly acted and incredibly written (duh) that I wept at the end, seated a few rows from the stage.

So, yeah, this last bit of this itty-bitty memoir is hyphenated with a love affair, but if we cast the *I Ching* over it, I think we'd find there's not much to sustain it.

So what have I learned? I've learned that if I remember to wrap God's pure cashmere cloak around me, a cloak that lets in cool breezes in summer and warmth from the softest-of-soft weaves in the winter, then it doesn't matter where I live or roam or visit or come back to.

That tender Cashmere Embrace is all that matters, all that IS, and if, as I'm living or roaming and I pass you, darling reader, on the Vagabond Way, and if I take some moments to magically, invisibly share that feel of God's cloak against your cheek, your shoulders, then all's perfect, for now.

And hey! I've got some ripe green figs in my knapsack. Wanna walk down to the river and share a few? Guaranteed we'll swap some good stories, fall back laughing, then stare at the water, maybe meditate or just lapse into a pleasant trance, and remember to be grateful, and to pull that cashmere Cloak around us.

In my mind the Cloak is pink.

ACKNOWLEDGEMENTS

I've fallen in love with key folks at Ozark Mountain Publishing, to whit the lady in charge, Nancy Vernon, who reached out to me across the query piles; the expeditious office manager, Brandy McDonald, and editor Debbie Upton who rendered my content smooth-as-silk.

I'd also like to thank the friends who've slung arms around my shoulders and hoisted me over the battlefields of life — being a vagabond, I search for them all over the frigging place, including — on Martha's Vineyard, Niki Patton who shines in these pages; my pal in Chilmark, Claire Ganz, who has put me up on her waterfront acres in the far country of North Chilmark; in New York Gwyn McAllister, also featured with bells and whistles in this memoir and, just down West 48th Street from her, photographer Robin Blair Riley plus, not lastly nor leastly my dear old high school bf, still in LA, Cynthia Renahan.

And never forgetting the Nadler boys, standup comedians and writers Marty Nadler and my darling son Charlie. Growing up with our kid, we used to all three hug and cheer ourselves on as "The Three Nadleteers". Marty and I split up a long time ago but we rejoined forces in the summer of 2020 and seem to be adept at getting each other through cultural traumas including January 6 2021 and other lame shit. Charlie has nurtured me through the gloom and doom of the last few years, God bless his dynamic and kindly soul.

And speaking of God and soul, I wish to launch a heart-felt tribute to the Self Realization Fellowship and my guru, the Paramahansa Yogananda, who has led me back to daily meditation, bolstered calm and peace and, one can only fervently wish, a coming life of Love, Wisdom and Bliss and all that good Stuff. My life as a hobo has taught me that home isn't here, as gorgeous as 'here' is, so I'll wait for the astral and causal planes and further instruction.

Finally, I'd be remiss not to send love to my late sister Cindy who died in February of 2020, I've always imagined of an undiagnosed early case of Covid, and my dear mum Trina who finally succumbed, in my arms, at her condo in Palm Desert CA, at the age of 100, 3 months and a few days. And finally but not lastly, I wish to thank my bro, Owen Mascott, once the baby of the family but now the able caretaker of our various odd business affairs; his braininess is evident and appreciated.

We'll see, we friends and family, where our next incarnations catch us up, as much as I'm praying for this to be the last go-round. If I keep meditating, Paramahansaji assures me, I'll burn up a lot of that crap karma. So will we all.

About the Author

Holly Nadler started her writing career at the age of 8 in the San Fernando Valley, when she received her first typewriter and tapped out a few chapters of a Nancy Drew mystery (not knowing you can't write someone else's series). As an adult she sold a couple of screenplays as well as scripts for prime-time TV comedies, including Laverne & Shirley and One Day At A Time. A move from LA to the Martha's Vineyard in 1991 led to 6 published books, notably Haunted Island, Ghosts of Boston Town, and Vineyard Confidential, as well as articles in national magazines such as Cosmopolitan, Lear's, and Women's World. She's spent enough years of travel, particularly in Europe, to learn how to live out of a suitcase. She's been married to — and divorced from — 3 lovely men and has a grown-up son, Charlie Nadler, professional standup comic like his dad, Marty Nadler. She writes for the MV Times and still putzes around as a vagabond. As she waits for someone to hand her a key to her next permanent home, she recommends, as coping devices, resilience, humor, and meditation.

If you liked this book, you might also like:

Beyond All Boundaries Book 1-3
by Lyn Willmott
The Oracle of UR
by Penny Barron
Dancing with Angel in Heaven
by Garnet Schulhauser
Life of a Military Psychologist
by Sally Wolf
The Birthmark Scar
by P.E Berg & Amanda Hemmingsen
A Quest of Transcendence
by Jolene & Jason Tierney
Being in a Body
By Victoria Pendragon

For more information about any of the above titles, soon to be released titles,
or other items in our catalog, write, phone or visit our website:
Ozark Mountain Publishing, LLC
PO Box 754, Huntsville, AR 72740
479-738-2348
www.ozarkmt.com

Other Books by Ozark Mountain Publishing, Inc.

Dolores Cannon
A Soul Remembers Hiroshima
Between Death and Life
Conversations with Nostradamus,
 Volume I, II, III
The Convoluted Universe -Book One,
 Two, Three, Four, Five
The Custodians
Five Lives Remembered
Jesus and the Essenes
Keepers of the Garden
Legacy from the Stars
The Legend of Starcrash
The Search for Hidden Sacred
 Knowledge
They Walked with Jesus
The Three Waves of Volunteers and
 the New Earth
A Very Special Friend
Horns of the Goddess
Aron Abrahamsen
Holiday in Heaven
James Ream Adams
Little Steps
Justine Alessi & M. E. McMillan
Rebirth of the Oracle
Kathryn Andries
Time: The Second Secret
Cat Baldwin
Divine Gifts of Healing
The Forgiveness Workshop
Penny Barron
The Oracle of UR
P.E. Berg & Amanda Hemmingsen
The Birthmark Scar
Dan Bird
Finding Your Way in the Spiritual Age
Waking Up in the Spiritual Age
Julia Cannon
Soul Speak – The Language of Your
 Body
Ronald Chapman
Seeing True
Jack Churchward
Lifting the Veil on the Lost

Continent of Mu
The Stone Tablets of Mu
Patrick De Haan
The Alien Handbook
Paulinne Delcour-Min
Spiritual Gold
Holly Ice
Divine Fire
Joanne DiMaggio
Edgar Cayce and the Unfulfilled
 Destiny of Thomas Jefferson
 Reborn
Anthony DeNino
The Power of Giving and Gratitude
Paul Fisher
Like A River To The Sea
Carolyn Greer Daly
Opening to Fullness of Spirit
Anita Holmes
Twidders
Aaron Hoopes
Reconnecting to the Earth
Patricia Irvine
In Light and In Shade
Kevin Killen
Ghosts and Me
Susan Urbanek Linville
Blessing from Agnes
Donna Lynn
From Fear to Love
Curt Melliger
Heaven Here on Earth
Where the Weeds Grow
Henry Michaelson
And Jesus Said – A Conversation
Andy Myers
Not Your Average Angel Book
Holly Nadler
The Hobo Diaries
Guy Needler
Avoiding Karma
Beyond the Source – Book 1, Book 2
The History of God
The Origin Speaks

For more information about any of the above titles, soon to be released titles,
or other items in our catalog, write, phone or visit our website:
PO Box 754, Huntsville, AR 72740|479-738-2348/800-935-0045|www.ozarkmt.com

Other Books by Ozark Mountain Publishing, Inc.

The Anne Dialogues
The Curators
Psycho Spiritual Healing
James Nussbaumer
And Then I Knew My Abundance
The Master of Everything
Mastering Your Own Spiritual
  Freedom
Living Your Dram, Not Someone Else's
Each of You
Sherry O'Brian
Peaks and Valley's
Gabrielle Orr
Akashic Records: One True Love
Let Miracles Happen
Nikki Pattillo
Children of the Stars
A Golden Compass
Victoria Pendragon
Sleep Magic
The Sleeping Phoenix
Being In A Body
Alexander Quinn
Starseeds What's It All About
Charmian Redwood
A New Earth Rising
Coming Home to Lemuria
Richard Rowe
Imagining the Unimaginable
Exploring the Divine Library
Garnet Schulhauser
Dancing on a Stamp
Dancing Forever with Spirit
Dance of Heavenly Bliss
Dance of Eternal Rapture
Dancing with Angels in Heaven
Manuella Stoerzer
Headless Chicken
Annie Stillwater Gray
Education of a Guardian Angel
The Dawn Book
Work of a Guardian Angel

Joys of a Guardian Angel
Blair Styra
Don't Change the Channel
Who Catharted
Natalie Sudman
Application of Impossible Things
L.R. Sumpter
Judy's Story
The Old is New
We Are the Creators
Artur Tradevosyan
Croton
Croton II
Jim Thomas
Tales from the Trance
Jolene and Jason Tierney
A Quest of Transcendence
Paul Travers
Dancing with the Mountains
Nicholas Vesey
Living the Life-Force
Dennis Wheatley/ Maria Wheatley
The Essential Dowsing Guide
Maria Wheatley
Druidic Soul Star Astrology
Sherry Wilde
The Forgotten Promise
Lyn Willmott
A Small Book of Comfort
Beyond all Boundaries Book 1
Beyond all Boundaries Book 2
Beyond all Boundaries Book 3
Stuart Wilson & Joanna Prentis
Atlantis and the New Consciousness
Beyond Limitations
The Essenes -Children of the Light
The Magdalene Version
Power of the Magdalene
Sally Wolf
Life of a Military Psychologist

For more information about any of the above titles, soon to be released titles,
or other items in our catalog, write, phone or visit our website:
PO Box 754, Huntsville, AR 72740|479-738-2348/800-935-0045|www.ozarkmt.com